AF812986

SOLITARY REFINEMENT

SOLITARY REFINEMENT

THE POWER OF ONE

JOHN McAVOY

WITH PAUL ZANON

pitch

First published by Pitch Publishing, 2026
1

Pitch Publishing
9 Donnington Park, 85 Birdham Road
Chichester, West Sussex, PO20 7AJ
www.pitchpublishing.co.uk
info@pitchpublishing.co.uk

© 2026, John McAvoy with Paul Zanon

The moral right of the author and illustrator has been asserted in accordance with the Copyright, Designs and Patents Act 1988

Every effort has been made to trace the copyright. Any oversight will be rectified in future editions at the earliest opportunity by the publisher.

No part of this book may be used or reproduced in any manner for the purpose of training artificial intelligence technologies or systems. In accordance with Article 4(3) of the DSM Directive 2019/790, Pitch Publishing expressly reserves this work from the text and data mining exception.

Set in Adobe Caslon 12/19pt

Typeset by Pitch Publishing

Cover design by Olner Design

Printed and bound in India by Thomson Press India Private Limited

The authorised representative in the EEA is
Easy Access System Europe OÜ, Mustamäe tee 50, 10621 Tallinn,
Estonia gpsr.requests@easproject.com

A CIP catalogue record for this book is available from the British Library

ISBN 978-1-83680-307-2

Papers used by Pitch Publishing are from well-managed forests and other responsible sources

MIX
Paper | Supporting responsible forestry
FSC® C010615

Contents

I would like to dedicate this book to everyone who has played a role in my life since being released from prison and helping me to become the person I've now become.

Acknowledgements

A big thanks to everyone who took the time to share some stories about my life. Special thanks to the following:

Toni-Ivana Awofeso

Simon Cox

Mike Crofts

Alex Croucher

Darren Davis

Chris Edmends

Huw Edwards

Ben Ellett

Alistair Elliott

Michele Glassup

Paul Gurney

Will Howe

Toby Hunter

Edgar Jörissen

Jasper Kain

Jay Kalama

Dr Phillip Lee

Karen Martin

Spencer Martin

Eleana Matos

Doug Mayer

Jamie McCall

Lisa Melvin

Dan Nastase

Christina Nathanail

Professor Rosie Meek

James Mitchell

James Montague

Aidan O'Flaherty

Ian Orton

Tom Otton

Sabina Mollart Rogerson

Claire-Marie Rozario

Dan Smith

David Smith MBE

Nimrah Sohail

Marek Sthalekar

Chris Thornton

Imogen Walsh

Chrissie Wellington

Terry Williamson

Foreword

The Power of Sport to Change Lives

I GOT the opportunity to join Nike many years ago, and I didn't hesitate for a second. I wanted to be part of the brand that brings inspiration and innovation to every athlete in the world – the company that invites all of us to make sport a daily habit, the company that tells us: *Just Do It.*

Just Do It. A simple, bold statement that speaks to all athletes – elite or everyday – and motivates us to take action without overthinking or excuses. I love *Just Do It.* I love sport. I believe sport has the power to change lives.

I was reminded of this truth in the most powerful way when I read an article about a man in prison who had just broken a world record on a rowing machine. His name was John McAvoy. The story told of his troubled youth, his time as a bank robber, his prison sentences. He came from an environment where sport wasn't 'cool'. It wasn't part of his identity. But in prison – the second time around – something changed. He found a gym, and in that gym he found a coach. And a rowing machine. And, eventually, he found something even deeper: he found true sport. It gave him a new identity. A new direction. A second chance. It was one of the most extreme examples I'd ever seen of how sport can transform a life.

As I was reading this story, I thought, *He should be a Nike athlete*. We've got to get him.

You can imagine how that sounded inside the Nike world: I was calling the Nike UK team and saying, 'Listen – I want you to seriously consider signing this man, John McAvoy. He's in jail … for robbing banks.' To their credit, they listened. They brought him in.

Not long after, we had a big Nike sales meeting coming up in the Netherlands. I asked John to come over and be part of my opening presentation. During my talk, I introduced him. 'Please welcome John McAvoy.' But with my clumsy English and a crowd full of Nike insiders, people thought I was saying 'John McEnroe', the legendary tennis player and Nike icon. Everyone stood up, expecting McEnroe. And then … they saw John. There was confusion – but by the end of the session, after hearing John's story, there was no more doubt. No one needed convincing. John McAvoy was a Nike athlete.

John has used sport to turn his life around – and now, he's using his story to help others do the same. He speaks to young people in schools, in prisons, in communities where sport is overlooked or undervalued. And when John starts talking, with his unstoppable energy, he connects. He inspires. He invites them to go for their first run, to step on to a rowing machine, to ride their bike to school instead of taking the bus. He invites them to let sport change their lives – as it changed his. He invites them to *Just Do It*. That's why I wanted John to be part of the Nike brand.

Later, John told me what that meant to him. He said, 'Nike's relationship puts a stamp of validation on me as an athlete. It takes me from being the bank robber to being an athlete, a motivator and a mentor for young people.' When he visits schools, some of the kids don't even care about his past in jail. They just want to know, 'How did you get sponsored by Nike?' That made me smile – because that's the power of sport. That's the power of belief. That's the power of a second chance – and the courage to take it.

Edgar Jörissen

(Former VP/GM for Nike Men's EMEA)

Chapter 1

Adjustment

'I help him, he helps thousands.'

—Terry Williamson

PEOPLE DON'T realise how hard it is when you get released from prison. My first flavour of semi-freedom behind bars was in 2011 when I went to HMP Sudbury, an open nick, where I was allowed out during the day, but had to be back by 5pm. Although I was outside of the prison grounds, I could only travel within a small radius, and because I lived too far from London, it meant I could never go home. So, on a Sunday, my good mate, Terry, who I met at the local Fitness First gym, would meet me and take me out for a Sunday meal at a restaurant in Burton-on-Trent, then we would see each other again in the morning at the gym. Terry was a massive help at the beginning, at a time when I had to disconnect from the world I was previously in; then when I was released in October 2012, nobody knew I'd got out apart from Terry, some really close family and maybe a couple of close mates.

Shortly after getting out, I remember driving up to Staffordshire from Kent on a Friday to Terry's and I hardly had enough money for petrol. I stayed a couple of nights and on the Saturday we made a £20 bet on the football, which I won. Then on the Sunday I was getting ready to leave and he said, 'You've forgotten this,' and went to hand me the £20. I said, 'No, mate.' I was very, very proud of that.

Although I probably could have done with the 20 quid for petrol, because I drove back to Kent with the red light flashing on the petrol gauge in my little 1.4 Renault, but my integrity was in the right place. A place it had struggled to be most of my life.

Financially, I don't think people really appreciated how hard it was at the beginning and how much self-belief I had to have in myself, especially as I invested so much into making it as an athlete, and this was way before Nike were on the scene. I was training people in the local park near the London Rowing Club in Putney, and the club would let me use the gym area, so I could train my clients at 5.30am, before I'd start rowing. I was only getting about £30 per hour, for a few hours, but it would just about give me enough money to live.

Then, there's other stuff that took me by surprise when I came out, which people wouldn't normally think would surprise somebody. Choice, for example. I was overwhelmed with it. When I'd go out for food, it wasn't just, say, rice, meat and veg. You could have what you wanted. I had to consciously get myself out of the old routines. For the first few weeks of coming out, I'd eat my food at the same time, because I was so regimented with the prison clock; then one day I said, 'Fuck this,' and ate whenever I wanted.

Then there were clothes. All of a sudden, I had the option of colours. In prison I couldn't wear certain colours, like black, white or red, so coming out and being able to wear what I wanted and pick what I wanted, when I wanted, was a novelty. It was those little things that you don't realise that have an effect on you.

When I was in prison, I was very defiant and was all about not showing weakness and being in total control of my body. I remember my uncle once telling me, 'One way you can avoid becoming institutionalised is by staying connected to the real world. Listen to the news, read the newspapers and make sure you remind yourself that prison is not your reality.' When I got out this time, when people saw me, they couldn't believe how well adjusted I was. The way I was able to converse with everyone and be happy and calm, but beneath the surface I still had barriers I was overcoming, like being tactile with people. I shook their hands, but that was it. I hated people touching me because of all those years of being patted like a dog behind bars.

Compassion was another one. When you're in an extremely violent place, compassion can take a different form. When I was in those maximum security prisons, I saw some horrible things. I'm talking hot oil getting chucked in people's faces, prisoners getting absolutely obliterated in the showers, getting stabbed up, then watching a lad getting stabbed in his arse multiple times and seeing his grey tracksuit bottoms go burgundy. The problem is that you become quite dismissive of it, because you see it all the time. Does being in a harsh environment of violence and hatred for many years have an effect on you? Of course it does. It has an impact on the way you perceive life. At the beginning I didn't see things from other people's perspectives, but now I do. If back then someone had an issue, I'd say, 'What's your problem? Just get on with it. Stop whingeing.' I had that mindset. Thankfully, that did wear off over time, and now, when someone treats me badly, I see that as a reflection of them, not me. But years ago, that would have triggered me off and my ego would have taken over, and I would have said, 'Who the fuck do you think you are talking to, like a piece of shit?' That was down to the people I grew up with, who drilled that into me.

Then there was trust and relationship values. When I was in prison, if I'd observed someone befriending a prison officer like I did myself with Darren Davis, I would have said, 'You're a grass. What are you doing in that corner talking to a prison officer? Don't come near me. I don't want to talk to you.' I remember people wore red armbands, which signalled to prisoners that they had the highest level of trust. They got to go to parts of the prison that the other prisoners wouldn't be able to access, like the staff room to make tea for prison officers, and get to walk around certain areas of the prison grounds. We would perceive anyone with a red armband as being prison informers and that they were giving information to the officers about what was going on in the prison. You wouldn't trust them. We used to call those red bands 'grass bands'. That was the psychology of how it was back then and my ego was a real problem. The reality is you realise that if you don't do what people ask you to do, you get sacked from your job, you can't make your mortgage payments and you lose your home, you can't make car payments and you lose your car. That's reality.

***

When my first book came out in 2016, I could have never imagined the amount of attention I was going to receive and the number of requests to do media interviews, which was a totally alien experience to me.

When I got asked to go on *Good Morning Britain* with Susanna Reid and Ben Shephard, I was jumping straight in at the deep end, because I'd never been on live TV before and never had any media training. The night before, I stayed at my friend's flat in Putney because I wanted to be closer to central London on the day, due to living out in Kent. They sent a car for me at 5am and we drove to the ITV studios on London's Southbank, turned up at reception and then they sent me upstairs to the green room. Shortly after, I got called to have make-up done and when I went back to the green room, the comedian Jim Davidson was sitting there with a newspaper and a coffee.

I said, 'Alright, mate.' He said, 'Alright. Are you on the show this morning?' and I replied, 'Yeah.' I then said, 'We've got a mutual friend,' and he asked, 'Who's that?' I gave the name of the person who I knew from one of the nicks and you could see the look on his face as he asked, 'How do you know him?' Up to that point I hadn't told him what I was on the programme for and said, 'I was in prison.' I then gave him a quick summary of my life and explained that I had a book coming out, and he said, 'Fair play to you, mate.'

As we were talking, someone came in and took me off to the studio and it wasn't how I thought it was going to be. It was a lot smaller and there were cameramen everywhere and a teleprompter there for the interviewers. They mic'd me up and, as the show went on an ad break, they turned on my microphone and I sat down, introduced myself to Ben and Susanna, and they said thanks for coming on and all that stuff. Then the show started and, as I was sitting there, they played a montage of Abu Hamza and numerous well-known prisoners I was locked up with.

As I was wondering how this interview was going to play out, I had a reflective moment looking at this montage, thinking how far I'd come in my life, sitting there on breakfast TV. The interview went well and they didn't drill me on anything, then when I came out Jim Davidson was still in the green room, and he said, 'Fair play, mate. I just watched that and you've got an incredible story.' He gave me his number and said, 'Shout if you need anything.' We shook hands, then I walked away and took my phone off aeroplane mode and the device just lit up with messages, including hundreds of notifications on Twitter which were really supportive.

That appearance opened loads of doors, and a couple of days later I went on Simon Mayo's *Drivetime Show*. Steve Coogan was there, reading his newspaper in the green room and I think he had a new TV show coming out and was there with a family member, and maybe his agent. I said a quick hello and then left him to it. The show itself was intense, because that was live radio and I had four minutes while having questions fired at me. You've got to be so on it and articulate in what you're saying when a show is that rapid-fire, but thankfully it went well and was another learning curve. From Simon Mayo I started going from one radio station to another and at one point I went to the BBC Studios seven times in four days.

As I already said, the majority of the comments and feedback I received were incredibly positive, but I did also get the odd bit of criticism; however, it genuinely never bothered me, because I always thought I was going to get more than I did. I always remember Terry telling me soon after being released that one per cent of people would criticise me. That's true, but the difference is, 1 per cent of ten is one thing, but one per cent of 10,000 is still one per cent, but it's a lot louder. I thought I was going to get way more people questioning why, as a convicted criminal, I'd been given this platform to speak, but I didn't. However, when it did happen, most of the time it was on Twitter and I got tagged on debates about me, or comments about a show I'd been on. That's when I quickly learned to post stuff, step away and don't engage, even if it's positive. Whatever people are going to say, they're going to say, and I can't please everybody.

The thing that was a bit trickier was when friends and family from my past saw me on television or listened to me on the radio. With a weaker head on me, I could have easily reacted in a different way. Let me explain.

I'm not a fan of red-top papers, and when we started doing PR for the first book I made it clear I didn't want to do any interviews with tabloids. Everyone accepted that. Then when the PR started, a broadsheet paper and one of the red-tops came back and I clarified my stance again. I was then told that if I refused the red-top paper in question, they would come after me and write what they wanted anyway. I stuck to my guns and explained I was happy to go with *The Times*, but not the other one. Then, on a Saturday evening of that week, I was driving over to my mum's from Putney and I got tagged in a Tweet. I opened the Tweet and it was this red-top paper and it had pictures of my uncle, Abu Hamza, you name it. It was exactly what I knew they would do, how they would frame everything and how they would sensationalise everything.

The red-top had released it to get a jump on the broadsheet who we were doing serialisation with for a Sunday release. It wasn't an absolute hatchet job and I guess it was positive with regards to them telling a story, but it was not the way I wanted it featured or written. I instantly knew that the people I wouldn't want to read this were going to read this.

A few days later, I went to visit my mum and she said, 'You've got some letters.' Normally, when I got handwritten letters, they were from people I knew in prison and I'd given them my mum's address, because it was always a consistent address for me. Believe it or not, the people I was in prison with were always supportive of what I was trying to do with my life and encouraged me to continue.

When I opened this one thick letter with loads of pages, I assumed it was someone from prison, but it turned out to be a family member. She said I was a disgrace sharing my story, and everything she said was all very, very toxic. This will sound strange when I say this, but reading that letter filled me with an immense amount of happiness, because I was so glad I no longer had that toxicity in my life. If I'd taken on board the contents of the letter from that day, this book wouldn't have unfolded the way you're about to read. If I'd tried to appease people that quite clearly didn't care about me and would rather I'd been a criminal than what I'm doing with my life today, I wouldn't have strayed far from the wrong side of the criminal justice system. I refused for my future to be written by them, ripped up the letter and chucked it in the bin. That was a pivotal moment in my life.

As I've evolved and I look back, I'm a very different person to the John that first came out of prison all those years ago and I'll probably be completely different in another ten years' time. Letting go of my ego is probably one of the biggest assets I developed when I came out, because my whole identity was so intrinsically linked to criminality, being respected and the honour that came with that. With my ego in the right place, it's time to take you through the last ten years of my life and the power of giving, listening and making opportunities for the next generation of youngsters.

Chapter 2

Every Day Is a School Day

> 'What I quickly learned about John is that his life experiences had a profound impact on him and he felt his purpose was to now give back to the younger generation. His generosity in terms of supporting individual students or groups of students to be able to access opportunities through his funding or by opening doors for them in the wider world changed all of their lives for the better. We will always be grateful to John for his kindness.'
>
> **—Simon Cox**

AROUND 2015, not long after I'd come out of prison, Simon Cox, the headteacher at Woodlands School in Basildon, Essex, saw me on a BBC newsreel, talking about my story and how I'd set world records behind bars. He said to his PA, 'Can you see if you can get this gentleman to come in and talk to our children, because I think he's got a great story for them to embrace.' Little did I know, but that visit would change my life.

When I set up my website, Terry used to manage it. Anything that was sent to me, Terry would receive it first. Any personal emails, he'd send them on to me to reply, but anything commercial, Terry would deal with. Up to this point, I'd come out of prison, had a type-A personality, wanted to be a high achiever and felt that being an athlete was going to right all the wrongs I'd done in my life. I was super-driven and focused, but that was all getting channelled into Ironman at that point. Then, when Terry got the email from Simon, he said, 'John. They've asked you to do a talk in a school,' which would turn out to be the first school talk I'd ever done.

I said to Terry, 'I really don't know what these kids are going to get out of what I'm going to say to them.' Terry said, 'I think you should go. It will be good for you.' I said, 'Okay, mate.' I drove up to Basildon, parked up and walked into the school, which was the first time as an adult I'd been in a school. The smells of the bleach, the certificates on the wall, it all brought me back to when I was a kid.

The receptionist asked, 'Can I help?' I said, 'I've been asked to do a talk.' She said, 'Okay. Sit here, because we need to take your picture and get your badge sorted out.' I was then taken to Simon's office and I instantly liked him. He's got a good heart, has amazing values, respects the value of his job and placed a big emphasis on sport to give these kids from disadvantaged backgrounds an opportunity to help them reach their potential, not just as athletes, but in other aspects of their lives.

He explained that there would be three talks broken up across the morning and afternoon, with a carousel of pupils coming in for 30 to 45 minutes. One group had become disaffected with education and were at risk of taking a similar path to mine at some point, and another group were students who were not necessarily going to school as much as they should due to bad attendance. Then the third group were elite performers. Simon had started to develop an elite programme and these were sportspeople who would benefit from listening to me talk about what it's like to train and the blood sweat and tears involved with reaching your goals.

I never really understood the power of my story until that day. Those kids listened to every single word I said. I was trying to get across to them what they could achieve for the rest of their lives and that everyone has an ability. You might not be good at English and maths, but you'll be good at something. However, in order to find that something, you need to have a very open mind, be willing to learn and put yourself in situations that challenge you, and don't let other people hold you back. I could really see I'd made an impact, because the number of questions that were fired my way afterwards was incredible.

The final group talk was in the afternoon, and once it was finished, I started heading back with Simon to his office for a debrief. As we were walking out, this young lad, George, came over and said to Simon, 'Sir. Can I talk to John?' Simon looked at me and said, 'Are you comfortable?' and I said, 'Yeah.' Simon replied, 'I'll stay in earshot just in case he says something that he's not supposed to.'

George was in front of me and said, 'I'm like you.' I didn't know what he meant, so I asked, 'What are you talking about, mate?' He said, 'My dad's coming out of prison and I don't want to go to prison like him. I don't want that life.' I replied, 'You've got something I didn't have at your age. You've got awareness. What do you want to do in your life?' He said, 'I want to work in sport, but I'm not a good athlete.' That school had one of the best sport teams in the UK and were beating most schools at everything. They really encouraged their pupils to get involved in sport, because they realised that sport could help them think outside of the box to flourish and grow, especially as many came from deprived areas. I said, 'You're in the right environment, with the right people. Even though you may not be an amazing athlete, you can work as a coach, a physiotherapist, an osteopath, a nutritionist. There's so many different things you can do in the sports world.' It was a really powerful five-minute chat and then we both left and went our separate ways home.

In 2018, I went back into the school for their assembly and did one of the first screenings of my Red Bull documentary. There were at least 200 kids and there were people from Red Bull there, but before we started I asked to see George because I knew he wasn't going to be at that assembly because he was in a different year. They pulled him out of his class and he couldn't believe it:

'Why have you asked to see me?' I replied, 'Because you made a massive impact on my life last time I was here. I just wanted to see how you were getting on.' He told me he was doing really well, training and was enrolling in a sports-related NVQ. I was so proud of him.

I left, and then a few months later Simon texted me to say, 'I think George is going through a bit of a tough patch. Would you jump on a call with him if I called you from my office now?' He called me up as I was driving and I spoke to him for about 30 minutes. He was telling me how he was struggling with the prospect of his dad coming out of prison, and I was doing my best to give him some hope and positivity.

Then a little while after, I found out about this touching story. George was doing his GCSEs, and in the middle of one of his exams he put his pen down. Simon saw him and walked over and said, 'What's wrong?' George replied, 'I can't do it, Sir.' Simon said, 'What can't you do?' He'd basically had a mental block for putting so much pressure on himself and Simon then said to him, 'George. What would John do right now?' George looked at him, picked his pencil up and started writing again. I don't know what grades he got, but he ended up passing his GCSEs. I'm not an emotional person, but I'll admit that did touch me.

You don't realise that just giving someone your time, not money or things, can make a massive difference to someone's life. Giving people your time and letting them be heard and letting them express themselves, then encouraging them is very powerful, especially when the person is perhaps not getting that elsewhere.

I then started thinking, *But all I'm doing is using words. Yes, you can inspire them, but what are you doing after that?* I didn't just want to speak, I wanted to create the vehicle for these kids to get them to think and behave differently and to make the best choices in life.

I went from being a guest speaker to an advocate and friend for the school and, as their elite sportspeople started to develop, I took an interest in a large number of their students who were doing incredible stuff outside school. I would come down and run some elite training sessions for them in the morning for about 250 young people for several different sports, and give bespoke mentoring for those who wanted it.

It's worth mentioning that when I first started going to the school there was no Nike at that point. The sequence of events was: do the school talk, my first book comes out and then Edgar gets in touch. But that didn't happen straight away. When I first went to that school, I literally had nothing. I hardly had any money and my life was just training, so when I went into the school, I wasn't financially in a position to help them on that front. I could only give time and barely had the money for travel.

I'd never mentioned this before, but when the book came out, I donated my very first royalty cheque to the school and that allowed Simon to pay for about 30 students to fly out to Italy to go and do a rugby training camp. I said, 'This is just between us.

I want to help you to help them.' At the time, someone on Twitter said, 'He only does what he does for recognition.' Simon jumped on the feed and said, 'You are very wrong. He's done loads of stuff for us that nobody even knows he's done.'

But when the book came out and then Nike came on the table, I was able to unlock opportunities, through kit and working with some of the athletes in the school. We did a few sessions where we were running around in PE and I showed them what it felt like to run at the pace of a three-hour marathon, which was quite funny, because they didn't realise how quick it was. They just saw three hours as a long time and thought it must have been quite slow, especially as they were teenagers and I was in my 30s, but as we started doing loops around this rugby pitch they quickly realised this old man had a lot of gas in the tank, as I started to lap them all.

There were hundreds of kids at that school who I had the pleasure to meet. I can't remember them all, but I'd like to mention a few. There was AJ, who was a super-talented sprinter and I first met him when he was eight years old. I brought the Nike team down, got him some spikes and kit, and mentored him. Then by the age of 13, I was very proud to be present to see him run 10.83 in the 100m, from a standing start without the use of starting blocks, which is insane. In the three or four years I worked with him, AJ was involved in the England setup for athletics and had an open offer from Saracens to play rugby. I asked Dan Smith at Nike if he could come down to Lee Valley

Athletics Centre, where Nike's elite sprinter group train, and he said, 'No problem.'

One of the head coaches, Marv, spent a day with AJ, and I went down, along with the PE teachers, because Simon had allowed him a day from school to engage with this experience. Marv said to me, 'He's an unbelievable talent.' At the time, I think his time was the second-fastest time ever in the UK for his age group over 100m. Marv identified that he needed continual discipline and guidance and at that age it was difficult for them to stay engaged and understand what it requires to be an elite athlete. At the time, Dwain Chambers was training and he had a chat with AJ and explained what it takes to be the very top in that sport, which was all healthy life-building blocks.

Then there was a gymnast called Halle Hilton, who went on to represent Great Britain and won two gold medals and three bronze at the Northern European Championships. At the time, Simon said, 'We've got this little girl here and she's very talented.' She was about 14 and a tiny sensational talent. I gave her some support of kit and stuff and got to meet her mum and dad, who kindly invited me to the O2 where she was doing a gymnastics event. I was like, 'Wow. What an amazing athlete.'

This final example, I only found out about at the time of writing. Emmanuel Iyogun was a really strong rugby player and I got on really well with him. Emmanuel was at a crossroads where he could have easily taken some different paths and maybe wasn't making good decisions at the time, so I spoke to him on an individual basis and did some sessions with him. What I didn't realise is that Emmanuel went on to play for Northampton Saints rugby union club in the Premiership and played in the Champions Cup Final in 2025. He still plays for Saints at the time of writing and has also had an England call-up. Again, I was so touched to hear that.

I also managed to get Simon and the kids down to Fulham Reach Boat Club. They drove a minibus over with about 16 boys and girls, some of whom had never been near water before and it was great to be able to take them out into a new environment and give them new experiences of what's out there in other communities. Some of them had never been out of Basildon before. In fact, I remember one of the parents contacting Simon saying they were worried about their child travelling outside of Essex, because they'd never been out the county, had been cocooned in their postcode and were scared to travel outside of that. The parents were clearly scared to travel and consequently that was projected on to the kids with the same mindset. Even though the water was a bit choppy that day, we still had a couple of hours with the instructors and it was great for the kids to be involved and get them to understand first-hand how rowing had changed my life. Everyone really enjoyed the day and I was also able to get about 15 of them to come down to the Oxford and Cambridge Boat Race with Simon for the day.

Doing those talks was a life-changing experience, because it made me think about what was really important to me. I'd gone from money being my god and ending up in prison to coming out and having this mindset of wanting to destroy people on rowing machines in hyper-competitive environments. Then once I'd done those talks and come away from that experience, it was like another moment of awareness in my life. Money and accolades were not the most important thing – the impact I could have on other people's lives was.

Chapter 3

One Size Doesn't Fit All

'I've been lucky to work with some of the most famous athletes in the world who go on those stages, who obviously garner respect and attention, but there's not many who held a crowd the same way John did on that day and continues to do.'

—Dan Fullelove Smith

Partner and Director at Summus Sports Group
(Former Head of Track & Field, Cross Category and Operations Sports Marketing, Nike)

DAN SMITH used to work at Nike UK in sports marketing and he was the one who initially reached out for Nike to sponsor me. He sent an email to my website, Terry picked it up, the dialogue started and a contract was offered. However, there's a backstory as to how I ended up signing that contract.

Dan joined Nike in 2012 and his boss left just before the Olympics, which meant he had to deal with a lot of the Olympic-focused work, which involved athletes, teams, clubs, federations, pretty much everything outside of football. So, everything from track and field, cycling, boxing, rugby, etc., dealing with people like Paula Radcliffe, Mark Cavendish, Mo Farah. Then one day he went into the office and he received an email from his boss, who received an email from his boss. The email landed in admin and it worked its way through down the chain until someone acted on it and that person was Dan.

At the time, there were kind of two buckets into marketing in Nike. Sports marketing, then brand marketing, which is community led, which is like the pulse of sport. I technically didn't fall into either bucket, but Dan was now tasked with trying to work out what to do with me. He contacted Terry, had a conversation with him and explained that he liked my story and would like to have an initial conversation with me.

I went with Terry to meet Dan, and although I might not have fitted squarely into their business model, he valued what I was doing with kids to help change their lives. Dan explained that if they could put the weight of Nike behind me, it could really amplify what I was looking to do and accelerate it. He said, 'Your average 14-year-old might not understand what Ironman is about or breaking an indoor rowing world record, but they understand what Nike is. Kind of, if you are sponsored by Nike, you must be cool.' They drafted a contract and that got me going on my journey with Nike in 2017.

When I went to Amsterdam, I went with Terry and Dan and had to do that presentation to announce myself in front of over 2,000 Nike employees. I was actually pretty calm. A lot of people find these things quite daunting and try to become someone they're not when put in that position. I must have been briefed about four or five times beforehand, with everyone giving me a different message about how to deliver a speech. Well, you can brief me 25 times, but I'll always get up and do what I do. I turned up in my joggers and told my story.

If you'd met me 20 years ago, I guarantee you would have come away with the same feeling of meeting me, as I am now. Certain characteristics of mine haven't changed, like communicating with people. That's a skill that my stepdad taught me when I was a kid, because, believe it or not, I was quite shy. He'd always put me in situations where I'd have to talk, like asking for things at the table both at home and at restaurants. He always told me, 'You can't just mix with criminals, you need to be able to mix with anyone and be more open to interact with them.'

I have to say, Nike have been an absolute dream to work with, and in all the years I've worked with them, I can only say incredible things about the way they work, their outlook on helping communities and, most of all, the faith they invested in me and continue to. In fact, all of my sponsors who have ever taken the time to be part of my journey and vision have never been anything but supportive. However, what I soon started to notice when going into the corporate world is the hierarchy, which can be very disarming to a lot of people, and when you're referring to some of the big brand names with tens of thousands of employees, it's a totally different game. Everyone looks up to the senior management like they're gods. I'm not one of those people, though, and I'd treat Edgar the same as I'd treat Dan or the person bringing in the teas, as would most people in Nike, because they have that healthy organic culture.

Outside of Nike, as I started to attend loads of meetings and functions, I also realised how quickly you can become invisible in these environments. Take for example when you're at a big function and you're speaking to someone and their eyes are scouring around the room, and they're talking to you but they're looking over their shoulders to see if there's someone more important to talk to other than you. I've seen people do it to me numerous times. They want something and when you don't give them what they want, they just tune out. That's why I think I've been able to get as far as I've done, because people can see I'm genuine about what I say. It's not like I rock up to this meeting and talk about all this charity work and say, 'Oh, by the way, that's my agent over there. Where's my fucking cut out of this?' Then my agent jumps in and says, 'John wants half the budget to help the kids.' That's not how I work and that's perhaps been to the detriment of me, if I'm honest, because I've probably given too much and some people do take the piss. I guess that was all part of my new learning curve in a new world.

For me, at the beginning, that's something I struggled with a lot, because I came from an environment of loyal individuals so had a very tight orbit of people around me. I can remember as a kid being with my uncle, Micky, in the south of Spain outside this restaurant and this guy came up to him and said, 'Micky! Micky!' My uncle turned around and said. 'I'm not Micky.' This guy said, 'Micky McAvoy?' My uncle said, 'No, mate. You've got the wrong person,' and turned around. He said to me, 'He's a piece of shit.' He wouldn't entertain anyone he didn't like. Whereas, when I entered the corporate world, all of a sudden I'm seeing people slagging people off, talking behind each other's backs, but making out they're mates with each other. That took me some time to really adjust to operating in this different ecosystem. I guess the big saving grace was that Nike didn't operate that way, so to see how other companies did operate just added to my toolkit in life.

***

In my previous life I was great at creating strategic plans and executing them. I was doing the same now, but with different focuses and outcomes and just needed some support to help me navigate and acclimatise to the corporate world. Cue Toby Hunter.

Toby started in Nike in 1996 and worked his way up to various vice-president roles and stayed with the company for almost 29 years. First time I met Toby was when I did that presentation on stage with Edgar in 2017. After finishing the presentation, I went into a room to sign copies of my book, as Edgar had kindly bought something like 750 copies and loads of people in that auditorium were gifted a copy as they were leaving. As all the books were being laid out, I was there with a felt-tipped pen and Toby came over and shook my hand. He didn't really speak much, but said, 'I think what you are doing is tremendous. We've got a few overlaps in our lives. Congratulations once again with how you've turned things around.' I said, 'Thanks, mate.' He told me a little bit about his background, then we shook hands and before he left I said, 'Hope we see each other again.'

Shortly after, Toby reached out to me on email and from that point we built up an amazing friendship. I think Toby appreciated that I wasn't from a corporate context and I'm mindful of what he did in the background to help me out, which I've always been immensely appreciative of.

Nike is a massive corporation, so you can easily fall through the cracks with things like contract renewals, because you can get to six months out and things can get shaky. That's unless someone is constantly positively manoeuvring you within the corporation, and that someone for me was Toby. I'm not going to chase people. It is what it is. If you want to work with me, then great, if you don't want to work with me, then don't. But in that world, if you haven't got someone constantly pushing and supporting your message and impact, 'Why is John's and his story not being leveraged for this,' or, 'There needs to be greater appreciation support all round for John,' then that relationship with Nike can and did start stagnating. I've got better at it now, but it's that question of: 'Commercially, what are you worth? What's your value as a person to the brand?' In and from 2017, that certainly wasn't my world and at the beginning I was a bit naïve too. Toby's always been a really good barometer, who over the years consistently reminded and challenged the Nike organisation to fully appreciate and understand the benefits to working with me and making a difference to young lives.

Years ago, I also remember having a conversation with one of the big executives at Nike about something similar. I signed that first contract, which got me through the door, but by the second contract I was training full-time, doing all these talks, because I wanted to give back, but I was overstretching myself massively and I was struggling to survive financially. I was spending about four grand a year on petrol, driving all round the country, doing all these talks for free. It wasn't sustainable, because I wasn't earning enough money, but I still carried on doing it.

I sent an email to this guy at Nike explaining that with what I was being paid, I couldn't afford to do all the work I was doing. He said, 'Leave it with me,' and within a couple of weeks they came back and offered me a different contract. They brought me into the offices in London and they basically doubled my salary. They said, 'We value what you're doing.'

Nike is a massive ship. The strategy comes down from a global level, then European level and there's hundreds of people involved in that process. Then you have to implement it. From the strategy stage to the implementation, it can take six months. With the likes of Edgar and Toby to help me, I never had to get involved in any of that detail. I carried on doing what I loved and they made sure the support from Nike was there to keep me going.

***

The Nike relationship continued to grow organically. As I was speaking to one employee, another would suddenly connect, and sometimes not totally in a work setting. Take Chris Edmends, for example. Very shortly after speaking with Dan, Chris heard me on talkSPORT doing a live interview with Andy Goldstein and Jason Cundy. It was November 2016, shortly after my first book came out and the interview was on about 10pm, lasted about an hour, but was split into four 15-minute chunks with advertising in between. This was my first proper long live radio interview, with no edits or anything like that.

Chris had worked for Nike for almost 17 years before eventually joining JD Sports and at the time was working down in London, despite living up north. On this particular day, he jumped off the train from his weekly commute back home, got in his car and started to listen to TalkSPORT for his 20-minute journey back. He'd missed the first part of the interview and was trying to piece together who was talking. Then when he got to his house, he could see his wife at the window, who looked completely burned out looking after their toddler for the last three days on her own. The look on her face was *Get off the phone!*, but he wasn't on the phone, he was listening to the radio and didn't get out the car, because my story was having a profound impact on him. He'd always been into running and cycling, so there was something there when I was talking about something to do with the triathlon that got his interest.

Then the interview finished and they mentioned my name and Chris thought, *Who? I've never heard of this guy. No clue who he is whatsoever.*

He went on to Instagram and still to this day he reckons it's the only ever time he's direct messaged someone who he didn't know. He said, 'I heard you on the radio and I work for Nike,' then a couple of days later Terry responded. We got a bit of dialogue going to and fro, and it's then, coincidentally, that we realised I already had something going with Nike which he knew nothing about.

I then ended up meeting him about three or four months later for a coffee in Soho, just down from Nike's office and we had a very long chat. We instantly vibed. By this stage Edgar had already contacted me, the contract had been signed and I was in the process of navigating the corporate matrix. I made Chris aware of all of this and we agreed it was all a bit mad that the two episodes of him and Edgar making an approach were totally unrelated.

Chris grew up in Rochdale, is rugged, had mates who went to prison, and he wasn't your stereotypical corporate person who got a marketing degree. We soon became really good friends and he's become super-supportive of me throughout my whole journey of working with Nike and outside of that. His networks have been incredibly helpful.

Funnily enough, I almost met the Edmends family before Chris sent me that message on Instagram. His mum was a schoolteacher and she reached out to me, without Chris knowing, to do a talk at her school in Manchester. However, the headmaster blocked it, because he didn't want me to talk to the kids because of my past. Small world, eh?

Over time things started to naturally fall in place with Nike and here's a nice example. In 2022 a lovely bloke called Jay Kalama had just moved into sports marketing, was managing Nike's relationship with Tottenham Hotspur and he'd heard my story on the radio. He wanted to bring in athletes and motivational speakers that would get the attention of first-team and academy players.

It's often more of a challenge to get the attention of the academy players, because they have more distractions than first-team players and you have a very small time window to get that attention, maybe ten or 15 seconds, whereas first-team players tend to be more focused and you might have about 30–45 seconds to get their attention. Then when you have that attention, you have to try to keep it, and that's where the speaker and their stories help.

I was in the Nike ecosystem and Jay reached out to the necessary person internally and explained what he was doing at Tottenham. Our schedules at the time were super-busy, but in the end we managed to get a time sorted out and I'm so glad we did.

I decided to bring a close friend of mine, Jack Burnell, who competed at the 2016 Rio Olympics in open water swimming. I first met Jack after the Olympics and he was sponsored by a company I was working with at the time called HUUB. While he was still a professional swimmer we met up in London and did a couple of training sessions together, then we became mates through a lot of common interests. He's mad into his football and is a big Chelsea fan. When I got asked to this event I thought it would be nice to get him to come along with me. I also asked him, 'Would you like to interview me on stage and then it would be good for you to meet the guys at Tottenham?' He agreed straight away. At the time he was working with Brentford Football Club as a sports psychologist, working with the players individually and as a group, so he was a perfect fit.

Jack's got an incredible story. He got disqualified in the Olympic final after punching this other swimmer who had pulled Jack's foot. If it wasn't for this guy, he could have most likely got an Olympic silver medal, but instead he got kicked out, lost his temper and, when he got out the water, live on telly to the BBC had an almighty rant, saying how shit the refereeing was, which went viral at the time. Jack had a very powerful story of not having self-control and the players got a lot out of his story.

Jack interviewed me on stage and I then spoke for about the next 45 minutes to the players. On the day, there were about 60 lads and ten staff, which included all the academy staff and academy director from Tottenham. There were a few senior first-team players and around 50 young people from the under-18 and under-23 teams. These were players from different races, but predominantly they were black kids. I'm a white, middle-aged guy, and if you look at this through a normal lens, I wouldn't be relevant to a young black kid in London. How are they going to relate?

Tottenham is still a very deprived area and one of the most underserved areas in London. Opportunities are lower than more affluent neighbouring areas like, say, Fulham or Chelsea, so it was essential to get their attention quickly and show them that I was on the level. I said, 'You need to focus on your football, I get that, you're an athlete, but always remember you are more than that. Kids look up to you and you can really make a positive impact in the world because of the role you've got.' At the end they all came over, super-respectful, and shook my hand, and then they started telling me some really powerful stories about their brothers, fathers, uncles and things that had happened to them.

The session lasted about 90 minutes, which included speaking with players afterwards and taking individual questions. Jay was able to get some incredible content from the day on to social media, which also landed on the Tottenham homepage. What a powerful experience.

However, 2017 had a lot more in store for me and it was a far cry from fanfares and sponsorship.

'I shouted, "Gun. Get down," as it was hard to know straight away what had happened. I then saw that a policeman had been seriously injured and a suspect shot. I took my bag off and said to John, "Hold this." I don't expect John is the bag carrier in many stories!

'I ran forward to PC Keith Palmer, while the group of boxers were all leaving Westminster Hall from an exit we should have been taking. Everybody was panicking and everyone starting to stream back into the hall, trying to escape the chaos. Tony, one of the boxing instructors, also came over the fence and came towards Keith to see what was going on and then we were joined by a couple more police officers.

'Initially, everyone saw he was hurt but perhaps thought they could administer relatively simple first aid and it would be alright. I've done two tours of Afghanistan and have been in quite a few casualty situations, and you get quite a lot of Team Medic training before going out. Team Medics almost exclusively focus on trauma-based injuries, such as gunshots, explosions and also knife wounds. I could see that Keith was going downhill quite rapidly and everyone around me was panicking, which is understandable in situations like this, but you need to get yourself back to a point where you're calm.

'I took a really deep breath and then said, "I need everybody to calm down," and everyone stopped talking. I then started to brief people on the process by which I'd be checking wounds and treating them, which is different to a normal first aid course, where you are taught DR ABC (look for Danger, any Reaction from the person, then check, Airway, Breathing and Circulation). With trauma wounds, it's catastrophic bleeds that you check first.

'I started doing the body blood check through his clothes and realised he had a very serious injury, directly to the heart. We tried to do everything we could to stem the flow of blood, but it was beyond our capabilities.

'I turned to one of the police who had a radio and said, 'You need to get a MERT here, straight away,' which is army terminology for a Medical Emergency Response Team. The policeman's said, "What's a MERT?" In London, that's called HEMS, which stands for Helicopter Emergency Medical Services. I said, "You need to get a helicopter here right now with doctors on it." Five minutes later, helicopters came over the bridge and started circling overhead, watching all the chaos, because a couple of people had also been knocked into the water, plus there were a lot of injured people on the bridge as well. It's a day I'll never be able to forget.'

—Mike Crofts

Chapter 4

22 March 2017

> 'Four people were killed and at least 20 wounded in London on Wednesday after a car ploughed into pedestrians and an attacker went on a stabbing spree with a knife before being shot dead close to the British parliament.'
>
> **(Source: Al Jazeera)**

I DID an interview with BBC Radio 5 Live in Manchester talking about how sport can play a fundamental role in communities to help young people. While on the show, they had Charlotte Leslie, who was a Conservative MP for Bristol North West, contribute to the narrative of what I was saying. She was a massive advocate of sport who also used to be a lifeguard before becoming an MP.

When the show ended, she contacted me on Twitter and said it would be great if we could meet up and perhaps do some work together moving forward. I said, 'Absolutely.' A few weeks before, Professor Rosie Meek had introduced me to a great guy called Mike Crofts and we had started to work together. I asked Charlotte, 'Could Mike from the 3Pillars Project come with me?' and she said, 'That would be great.'

Here's a bit of background about Mike. Before starting 3Pillars, Mike served in the army for eight years and did two tours of Afghanistan. His first job after leaving the army was working for Goldman Sachs and one day, while sat there in the bank, he had a moment of: *What the hell am I doing here? I didn't leave the army to sit in a bank and report someone's transactions from three months ago to the FCA. What an utter waste of my life.* In the meantime, some money had come in for his 3Pillars Project and he resigned from Goldman Sachs to set up the charity.

The 3Pillars Project delivers rugby into prisons and it's all about helping young men with positive role modelling. Someone Mike was initially setting a project up with, Rebecca, a barrister at a big American firm, had read about me in an article around 2016, and they were interested to work with me. However, they had to be sure I wasn't just another story that someone in the media had cooked up to make me sound more than I actually was.

One day I got this call from this barrister. We had a chat and then I met her in person in Putney. What a lovely person. We spoke for a couple of hours about prisons and reform, then she said, 'I'd like to introduce you to Mike Crofts.' I said, 'Great.'

Shortly after, she emailed Mike and said, 'I've just spoken with this guy, John McAvoy and he's the real deal.' They ended up putting my story in their course handbook as an example of someone who had done quite a meaty sentence, but completely changed their thought pattern, which is a strong part of how 3Pillars works – using sport to build relationships and try to change some conventional thinking about how people perceive their lives. I did that, pretty much in isolation.

One of my earliest meetings with Mike was going to Wormwood Scrubs to share my story and life experience to a group of prisoners who were part of the 3Pillars Project. We went through reception and they gave me a tour, took me up to the gym and then Mike said, 'Do you want to go on the landings, because there's a couple of prisoners on the landings who can't come on the talk today?' I said, 'Let's go.'

Mike was a keyholder, so we headed to the landing. We walked out the gym, got to the landings, then had a walk round. It was a very surreal experience, because firstly it filled me with a lot of sadness to see humans locked up like that. All that potential just sitting in these coffins, in that grey, bland environment, while my life was so wholesome and colourful. It took me back to me being in that situation all those years ago.

As we were walking down the landings, everyone was screaming, which was yet again another reminder of my previous life. There was a guy Mike wanted me to meet who had just been sentenced and had got a life sentence with a 20-year tariff. I went into his cell and it was just me and him chatting while sitting on beds facing each other. He asked, 'How am I going to get through this?' I could only give him some advice of what helped me and said, 'You have to take every day as it comes, but you have to remember that this is not forever. You've got to look at this as an experience of growing and development and bettering yourself.

You can educate yourself, go to the gym and get fit. You need to look after yourself both mentally and physically. Even though it's going to be a long time, you can utilise it. I spent ten years in a place like this and managed to get to the life I have today. I know you have a longer sentence than me, but it's still doable.'

We sat there for about half an hour, he made me a cup of tea and we just chatted and chatted. It was something I wasn't expecting. I thought I was going into the gym to talk to a few guys about the 3Pillars Project, but instead I had this really powerful moment in that cell, as this guy looked at me like this source of hope. I came out the prison, which was only about 25 minutes home, and all I did was think about how lucky I was. The fact that I was just able to get up and walk out of that place and not be stuck there, like I was all those years before.

The second meeting I had with Mike was going up to HMP Lowdham Grange. Here's how that one came about. I did an event at global sports company IMG in London to their staff and, during that talk, someone said to me, 'Why did you decide to do Ironman?' I said, 'Because, when I was in prison at Lowdham Grange I watched *Transworld Sport* on Channel 4.' At the end, someone came up to me and said, 'You do know we made that, we own *Transworld Sport*?' I said, 'I had no idea.' He then said, 'Do you want to be in one?' I replied, 'Yeah.'

Subsequently, *Transworld Sport* did a feature on me in preparation for an Ironman race. Then, off the back of that, Darren Davis came on my episode to do some filming and the guy who made it said, 'It might be we could get access to Lowdham Grange to see the work Darren is doing with other prisoners.'

I asked Darren, then Darren asked the prison, and they said yes. A second episode was filmed on Darren Davis and there were a couple of other prisoners who took part, who had similar stories to me, such as Kane Mousah, who was an MMA fighter before he went to prison. He got caught with a mate one night with a gun in the car, got a nine-year sentence, but while in prison kept training. He was released and restarted his career as a fighter, and he now lives in Dubai doing positive things with his life. Anyway, I messaged Kane and said, 'Do you want to go to Lowdham Grange and take part in this episode of *Transworld Sport*?' He said, 'Yeah.'

We went in, did a talk to the prisoners and it was more about Darren and how he'd changed mine and Kane's lives, talking about how Darren had set up this sports facility in the prison to help prisoners get through their Level 3 Gym Instructor qualification. Then shortly after, I asked Mike Crofts if he wanted to come up and look at Lowdham Grange to meet Darren and see the work he does, and if there was an opportunity for Mike to start working in that prison.

Coming back to Charlotte Leslie. In March 2017, we met up outside the Houses of Parliament and we went inside the government offices, which was a big shiny building on the opposite side of the road from Big Ben. We had this relaxed chat with Charlotte in this cafeteria and she was talking about various projects. We discussed what Mike did. When we were about to leave, she said, 'Would you like to come over to an event this afternoon, with the Boxing All-Party Parliamentary Group? It's quite informal and it's about boxing in the communities.' I didn't have anything to do that afternoon, nor did Mike, so we said, 'Sounds great.'

We walked with her down this tunnel, which went under the road and ended up in the main, old historic Houses of Parliament building. There we were on this veranda area overlooking the River Thames and there's loads of people from the boxing world. From local boxing clubs, through to top guys wearing the GB boxing kit, such as Frazer Clarke, who were getting ready to take part in a tournament. A boxer called Mo Ali spoke really well and talked about how boxing changed the course of his life. There was also a boxing coach there called Tony Davis, who was one of Mike's PTIs when he was at Sandhurst, ten years before. The whole day was serendipitous.

The events started early afternoon and people were talking about boxing and how it had impacted their lives, and then on the veranda part, there was a photoshoot of young boxers with their coaches on the pads. It was a nice wholesome couple of hours, then it all started wrapping up, and we started saying goodbye to everyone.

We then went to walk back out of the parliament area, but before we did, Mike said, 'I need to get my jacket.' We went to get his jacket and then walked through all these corridors to get out. We took a route that guests wouldn't normally take, but with Mike having previously worked for an MP called Dan Jarvis, he knew his way around and we ended up taking a route that brought us out into Parliament Square where all the MPs had pulled up.

As we were walking out, we heard loads of shouting and screaming and Mike said to me, 'Let's go and see what's going on.' We picked up our pace and, as I looked up, Mike was to my left and I saw someone running towards parliament, looking like they were being chased, with loads of shouting going on. My initial reaction was: 'It's a protester.' I thought someone was dressed up as a policeman, wearing a fluorescent jacket and trying to break into parliament through the car park area, as an individual was trying to catch him up. It turns out the individual was fatally attacking a police officer.

As we walked into the square, the whole event unfolded in front of us. The guy in the fluorescent jacket dropped to the floor about 30 metres away from me and suddenly an armed police officer got out of his car and I heard all this screaming. The police shouted, 'Stop, stop, stop,' then seconds later it was 'Pop, pop, pop, pop, pop', as all this gunfire started. Mike shouted to me, 'Get down. It's gunfire,' but my brain wasn't processing what was happening in front of me. It was so surreal.

There was a car near us and we both got down next to it. Within seconds police appeared from everywhere with machine guns, running to the scene. Mike gave me his bag, got up and walked towards what was happening, and then the police kind of scooped everyone else up who was in that car park and bundled them into this building that was attached to parliament.

We were in these corridors and the police were saying, 'You need to get in these rooms.' Someone else said, 'We think it's a terrorist attack and we think parliament is being attacked from both ends.' It was chaos. There were people running into parliament from all sides and there was a lot of confusion. I ended up being in this massive old meeting room, as you'd imagine in Westminster, with leather chairs and a big desk in the middle.

They locked us in this room with all these random people who had been swept up at the same time, with a load of MPs, including Alex Salmond and David Davis, but you also had builders, who were doing work in there. We were all locked in there for hours and started watching the TV up on the wall, and that's when it became apparent what had just happened outside. Up to that point, I'd seen what had happened, but I had no idea that the policeman had been stabbed.

I was now putting the pieces of the puzzle together and the bloke that got shot was obviously the terrorist. I started speaking to some of the people in the room and told them that I saw what happened, and more and more people started coming over, asking me to tell them my recollections. There was a security expert in the room and he said, 'The integrity of the building has completely gone, because people should not be mixing in this room together like this.' You had a builder with the leader of the SNP, all locked in together, with nobody having the correct passes or, like myself, with no pass at all. We were in there for a good couple of hours and then they let us out and armed police took us over to Westminster Abbey, which was just across the road, and walked us back through the car park where the incident had happened. There were more helicopters buzzing over parliament, and I remember thinking, *Fucking hell.* By this point, it was about 7pm and we were just sitting around on the stairs, the chairs, wherever you wanted.

They finally let us out about 10pm and it was like a football match, where the crowds empty out of the stadium. There was a massive line of police officers with notepads and pens and you had to walk up to them and answer four questions. 'What's your name? What's your address? Date of birth? Did you see anything?' I answered the questions, and when I said, 'Yeah, I saw something,' he asked, 'What exactly did you see?' I replied, 'I watched the policemen shoot the terrorist dead.' I don't think he was expecting that. He was writing all this down, and he said, 'You're a priority witness. The police will reach out to you in the next 24 hours for an interview.' I said, 'Okay,' then left.

It was a very clear evening, but it was strange as everything was on lockdown. It was like a scene out of the film *28 Days Later*. I started walking back towards Putney and it was very eerie as the roads were silent and empty, hardly any people walking about. I then started to process what had happened, and thought, *If this guy was wearing a suicide belt, I would be dead right now.* I felt very lucky to be alive.

I walked back to Putney and the next day I went to meet Mike Crofts in a coffee shop in Putney, because firstly I had Mike's bag and, secondly, we wanted to have a bit of a debrief. The episode really impacted Mike and he was a bit shell-shocked, because it's not every day you see someone die in front of you like that. We spoke about the incident and I said, 'This is a tragic, horrible thing that's happened, but what you did was amazing. People will want to hear about it and there's an opportunity for good to come from this.'

That convinced Mike to do a news article and talk positively about Keith Palmer and what had happened. Normally, Mike's reaction would have been to be very low key, but there was an MP involved with the event, who was clearly feeding some lines to the press and the narrative was going in the wrong direction. It was important for Mike to say something because a policeman and four innocent civilians were murdered on the bridge. It was important for him to put the person who had been standing in the gates to try to stop this guy coming through into the forefront of the story, which is why he ended up going on to *BBC Breakfast* and doing an interview talking about Keith Palmer's bravery. Mike was awarded the Royal Humane Society's bronze medal and a commendation from the Commissioner of the Met Police for his heroic actions.

Me and Mike finished our coffees, said our goodbyes and then later on that afternoon the police officers called and said, 'We'd really like to interview you today if you feel up for it.' I said, 'Yes. Would you like me to come to a police station?' They said, 'We've interviewed a lot of people today who have been badly traumatised by the events yesterday and we'd rather do it in a neutral place where you feel comfortable, as you're a witness and not a suspect.' I said, 'Okay. Come to London Rowing Club.'

They came over about 6pm that same evening and I took them upstairs to the members, part and we did an interview. They wanted to see my phone, because I'd taken a video of the aftermath. They asked me a few more questions and then switched the tapes off. What he did next took me by surprise. He put his hand out and said, 'Can I shake your hand?' I shook his hand and he said, 'Me and my colleague cannot believe how you've managed to turn your life around.' I said, 'What do you mean?' He replied, 'Before we interview people, we have to do a national record check on our database. You were in a high security unit, weren't you?' I said, 'Yeah.' He then started reeling off all these names of terrorists and said, 'I nicked them when I was in the anti-terrorism unit. The chances of you, after being with all those people, to now being caught up with that terrorist attack is tiny.' The irony of me being there that day didn't get lost on me, considering what my life used to be. That event brought me there that day to experience that sense of extreme and horrific violence that you can enact on another human being.

I started to process what had happened over the following days. There was a man who had got completely lost in life and, by being lost, he had attached his focus on to something that was super-negative and toxic. There was a similarity between him and myself as a young man and looking up to the wrong people and wanting the wrong things out of life. Obviously, me and that guy were very different in the way we conducted ourselves, though. I decided to attack the system through monetary gain and had a hatred towards the state and the system, and he chose a much more violent approach to back up his aims and beliefs.

I spoke with Mike Crofts about this, the importance of the work we do and why it's important to give people positive role models and give them opportunities, because if you don't, someone else is going to fill that vacuum. For me, in the week that followed, that day reminded me so much why the work that we do is so important. I'm sure that if someone else had come into that man's life when he was in a vulnerable place and directed him into something positive, he wouldn't have done what he did that day and killed that policeman. It motivated me more than ever to think of ways of continuing the work I was doing.

Chapter 5

Parliamentary Procedure

'John delivered this amazing speech and you could see everyone thinking, "This guy was a proper criminal." Not someone just stealing to feed a drug habit, this was a hardened criminal who had reformed through the power of sport. It was brilliant. He was brilliant. What John didn't know was that the impact it had on staff of the MOJ [Ministry of Justice], because they are just constantly just polishing turds. All of the problems the MOJ have at present are the same they had ten years ago. Constantly overfilled prisons, drugs and, in some cases, corrupted prison staff. The mental illness burden and recidivism were also both dreadful. Rarely something positive to deal with, which is actually quite tough for the staff to work in that environment with that type of responsibility. Then along comes this meeting.

'He's leading by example. His very being is so powerful to kids thinking of taking the easy route to a bit of extra cash and other superficial popularities in their community. He embodies that sentiment of: "No. I did that. Decent human beings do this instead." What he was like and what he is like now speaks volumes. He almost doesn't need to speak.'

—Dr Phillip Lee

Former Parliamentary Under-Secretary,
Ministry of Justice

I FIRST met Professor Rosie Meek in 2016. At the time, she was Head of the Law School at Royal Holloway University of London and she'd started up a Master's degree in forensic psychology.

I was on BBC Radio 2 with Simon Mayo and several others, and that's probably how she became aware of me. Also, one of her colleagues was a member of my cycling club. Rosie sent me an email and said, 'I'd like you to come and talk to my students. A lot of them are training to be practitioners to work in prisons and I think it's really important that they hear your story. I can't pay you, but I can give a £50 donation to a charity of your choice.' I said, 'That's fine. I'd like to choose Fulham Reach Boat Club please.' At that point, I really didn't have much to my name, but the value of what she wanted me to do went beyond monetary value.

About four weeks later I went down and I remember walking through the green courtyard of the university and seeing this super-impressive building. If memory serves me correctly, I think they were going to film Harry Potter there at one point. Then I walked into the building itself, got a bit lost and was knocking on office doors. Next thing, someone said to me, 'Rosie Meek's waiting for you,' and walked me to the top floor. It was the first time I'd ever met her in person and we started having a chat. Psychology fascinates me and I was asking loads of questions about what she does and why she does it, then she took me downstairs and introduced me to a guy called Nick Hardwick who was a professor there as well as being chair of the Parole Board, but he had also previously been Chief Inspector of Prisons.

I gave this talk to these psychology students about the importance of sport in prison and how it turned my life around, and I think they found the aspect of change very fascinating. The concept of how it's possible in people and how you can redirect someone's energy to something positive from an initial negative starting point. It was the first time I'd spoken to university students and was very mindful of where I was putting my hands and being very self-aware, because I assumed they were analysing everything I was saying and whether my body language was aligned to that. They were used to learning about people with psychopathy and sociopaths, so when I was speaking I was thinking, *I wonder what they're making of me?* Thankfully, it went really well.

Afterwards, Rosie gave me a copy of her book, *Sport in Prison*, which had come out a couple of years earlier. We spent a long time talking about these issues in the prison system that we were both so passionate about. We built up this amazing rapport and have become very good friends ever since. It's like we're like kindred spirits and are often brought out as a double act, where one talks about the academic side of things and the other talks about their experience. Little did I know, we were about to demonstrate that in just a few months, but in slightly different surroundings.

***

From court chambers for life sentencing, to speaking at the chambers in the Houses of Parliament. I was having another one of those 'pinch me' moments. Here's how that opportunity came about.

I'm not big into politics, so when Terry mentioned to me in spring of 2017 that an MP called Dr Phillip Lee had been in touch and wanted me to meet him at the Houses of Parliament, my first, though, was *Who?* Here's a little bit about Phillip, why he wanted to chat and how this meeting came about.

Despite being known as an MP, Phillip has an amazing knowledge of sport and was something of a natural sportsman himself. He ran the 100m in 11.5 seconds, got involved with football from the age of six, was scouted at 11 for West Ham while playing for his district side, but unfortunately his parents didn't want him to turn pro.

From a young age, Phillip understood the values of sport in society and knew it had personally been good for him. As far as politics goes, it was always there in the background for him from a young age, and if they had those high school yearbooks in Britain, they may have said, 'Yeah. He'll do something like that. He'll want to get sport into society to help create a better society.'

When he eventually got into politics, what he realised very quickly was that there were very few people who were sporty or who had sporting interests. He'd be sitting in a room with these other MPs and they didn't understand his vision. Then when he got a ministerial role, he realised that most of what he was dealing with was mental illness, both within the prison population and the MOJ. He thought, *Okay. I'm going to try and use sport to help.*

He tried for six months to get a first meeting, after various people tried to block it, but then he eventually got the go-ahead. He then thought, *How's this going to work?*, because most meetings in government are like watching paint dry and are not particularly inspiring. He wanted someone who could personify what he was trying to do and the values he was trying to tap into. While blindly searching on Twitter, he came across this name, 'John McAvoy.' He straight away instructed his government office: 'Could you reach out to this character and see if he'll come in?' That's when Terry received that email.

A lot of people said to me, 'Why would you want to go to somewhere that took ten years of your life?' but I didn't see it like that. Those ten years I spent in prison, I wouldn't change. I learned so much about myself and met so many fascinating characters that I got to interact with. When that email came in, I realised how much my life had changed and I wanted to recreate the narrative of my life and go down a different journey from what it was years before. Then when I went into the MOJ, the irony of all the resources and manpower to keep me locked up for all those years and to prevent me from escaping never got lost on me and it didn't get lost on Dr Phillip Lee now, who wanted me to help change the criminal justice system in the UK. It was a proud moment, not a bitter one, even if I was a bit apprehensive of the unknown. On a side note, I think Phillip should have been the prime minister because he had compassion, morals and he was coming from a place of care as an operating GP. If he had become more powerful in government, I think Britain might have been in a better position.

That meeting was in spring 2017 and I won't lie, it was surreal to be at the MOJ building. Due to the level of security I had when I was in prison, everything had to go through government level to sign it off, which meant it would have come out of the MOJ building.

On the day of the meeting, I turned up wearing a Nike tracksuit and me and Terry headed to the ninth floor of the MOJ to Phillip's office. The problem was that this particular floor is a secure area and because I was on life licence, I wasn't allowed in. Thankfully, Phillip had some weight and was able to get special permission to get me upstairs.

I walked into his office and that first meeting consisted of me, Terry, Phillip and his political aide. I said, 'I can't believe I'm here, in a Minister of Justice's office.' He replied, 'I've been reading about you and I think you might be able to help in terms of trying to get something started. Would you turn up and tell your story?' I said, 'Yeah. No problem.'

We had a 45-minute chat where Phillip asked me questions about my life, and when I started to talk about discovering a Concept 2 rowing machine behind bars, we soon found we had some common ground. It turned out he could bash out about 6min 45sec for 2,000 metres on a Concept 2 at his peak, but it also turned out he was a late starter with swimming, like myself. He only learned how to swim when he was 25, mainly because his dad was terrified of water and his mum could hardly swim.

Phillip explained his idea to me, which was basically to get me in front of some big names in the world of politics and sport and talk about the merits of sports in a prison setting. The only problem was that he had no idea how I was going to present my story at the session at the MOJ. This could have gone seriously pear-shaped, but Phillip remained positive and set about trying to get people to this first meeting.

You have to remember my distrust of the establishment and I also didn't know Phillip from Adam. Phillip was bringing a load of people in and I was one of them, but it was clear within the first ten to 15 minutes of just the three of us being in the room that Phillip was genuine. It wasn't just a tick-box exercise for him and that he had a pot of money and was going to create some quangos and all that shit. He genuinely wanted to do something positive. Probably the first politician I've ever liked.

About a month later, I was invited back to the MOJ and it was like a round table they were doing. Phillip wanted to commission a report, which would review the criminal justice system and how using the power of sport could improve things. I didn't know who was going to be there when I turned up and you can imagine my shock when I walked into this tiny little room at the MOJ and there was Professor Rosie Meek sitting opposite me, then David Dein was at the other end of the table, plus you had all these people who headed up all various charities and who were all influential within the sports industry, like Street Games, and UK Active, represented by Huw Edwards, who went on to become CEO of that organisation.

Phillip did his brief, with the usual 'thank you everybody for coming today, it's great to have you here,'-type thing. Then he said, 'Before we start, I'd like to ask John McAvoy to tell his story.' This was maybe the second time I'd done public speaking and I gave a five-minute presentation about how sport changed my life. David spoke next and the session lasted an hour and a half.

Neither I nor Phillip expected to see David Dein at that meeting. You could see people in the room thinking, 'What's he doing here?' Everyone knew him on television as the man who sold Arsenal Football Club and was one of the founders of setting up the Premier League, but I had no idea that he did a lot of talks with young people and he was also on the speaking circuit going to schools. When he started talking about the work he did going into prisons and speaking to prisoners, that impressed me.

cafeteria, but very high end. You've got waiting staff coming up to you as you sit on these leather chairs. 'Would you like some jam on your scone, Sir?' That kind of thing.

There we are chatting and I looked over my shoulder and I saw David Blunkett there with his dog. The irony. What happened was, my sentence was ruled as unlawful by the European Court of Human Rights and the government lost. I'd got a discretionary life sentence, which meant it was at the judge's discretion. Let's say, for example, I was caught in somewhere like Manchester or Liverpool, the judge there might have given me ten or 15 years for the same offence, but because I was in London and I got a high-profile crime judge, he gave me a life sentence at his discretion. The European Court of Human Rights said, 'No. There has to be a consensus of XYZ. This is what constitutes a life sentence. You can't just give it at discretion.' Some sentences have set timeframes and others are pot luck.

The government lost and, when that happened, they then brought in IPP (Imprisonment for Public Protection), which was down to Blunkett. It was also known as the 99-year sentence and that was even worse than the sentence that I'd originally been given! It was basically a rebranded life sentence and, as these judges started handing them out, it caused major problems in the prison service, because it put all the accountability of when these people got released on to the parole board. Then, there was no reoffending behaviour courses for prisoners to go into, to demonstrate they were no longer a risk. It was a total shambles.

Prisoners were sitting in prison waiting for their tariffs, while the prison system bottlenecked up.

As a result, David Blunkett was very hated in the prison system, as you can imagine. Now, here I was, having tea with Tanni while Blunkett's over my shoulder as we're discussing how to improve opportunities for young people in society. The irony. Especially in the House of Lords. The setting was poetic.

So 2018 was a year that really made me take stock of where I was and how I'd got there. Even outside of the likes of 10 Downing Street and the House of Lords, I'd have constant reminders of how far I'd come. Even now, when I go back to London, I know the places to go and not go, as I don't want to see people from my past and I don't want to engage with them, but sometimes you can't avoid it. I remember going to the George Groves versus Jamie Cox fight in October 2017 at the Wembley Arena, and I was sitting in the heavens in terms of the seats, when this guy walks past me who I was in prison with at Lowdham Grange and we got chatting. What's the chances of that? Then, not long after, I was watching Anthony Joshua fight at the Principality Stadium in Wales in 2018, when again the kid standing next to me had been in HMP Full Sutton for six years. It wasn't just a case of saying I'm not going to speak to people. No. It was hard. Really fucking hard, because there were so many people I shared so many amazing memories with and they were so loyal to me and so good to me, but I knew I needed my life to go down a different road.

Final example for 2018 was in November. I was up at the Manchester Arena in the build-up to Tony Bellew versus Oleksandr Usyk. I'd been asked up to do a talk by Toby Hunter from Nike and I was with a load of JD Sports senior directors, and Tony Bellew was doing a talk on stage after me, because he was a JD athlete at that time. Then about two weeks later I was sitting just behind ringside, getting ready to watch Bellew against Usyk and, sod's law, there was this guy who was a really notorious criminal in Liverpool for drug trafficking and I'd been in prison with him. I looked over, he looked at me and he came over and said, 'Oh my god! Lad. What you doing up here?' We hadn't seen each other since being in prison and at the beginning he was talking to me like I was John from 2006. I was standing there with the senior directors of JD and I explained that my life was so different now and what I was now doing with myself. He was in the middle of some crazy war up in Liverpool, but I explained that I didn't want to know about that stuff anymore. He was a funny, down-to-earth person who was really intelligent, but who also came from a family of crime and chose to go down the wrong path, which was quite sad, because he could have done anything he wanted in his life. It made the Open Doors project and everything I was doing with the government so much more important.

***

Open Doors was initially piloted in the summer holidays of 2019, as ukactive had the opportunity to work with Sainsbury's, who had seen the opportunity and opened up to something like 75 sites before Covid. Then when I came on board with Nike, it became a bit more focused in its approach. It was a great opportunity to look at how to combat holiday hunger and inactivity, with the opportunity to provide kids with safe access to safe spaces, a meal during the day and a breadth of different activities across traditional sport to participate in. Nike had some priority areas of London, Manchester and Birmingham, and ukactive started to open up the schools in partnership with the respective local authorities. There was social connectivity, the kids weren't sitting at home, instead they were out with their mates. The project ran two days a week, four hours a day and the programme was delivered and evaluated by Dallaglio RugbyWorks, looking at three focus areas, which were engagement, integration and achievement.

From having both feet firmly on the ground, it was now time to take to the water.

Chapter 7

Making Waves

'I think Boats Not Bars would have been possible without John, but I don't think it would have happened when and how it did, without his inspiration and education. Me personally, I don't think I would be working in the criminal justice system if I hadn't of spoken with John initially. Becoming an Ironman doesn't have to be your goal, but whatever it is, it's just as possible and John is evidence of that. His story gives credibility and inspiration to the whole notion that getting involved in sport can actually become your focus, your therapy and your daily uplift.'

—Imogen Walsh

ON THE back of the Dr Phillip Lee stuff, Terry wrote a business plan to go into prisons to do triathlon with him, myself and Darren Davis. Unfortunately, it never happened, but thankfully several other initiatives did unfold.

In 2018, I became an ambassador for Fulham Reach Boat Club in Hammersmith. They work with about 12 state schools and five private, within the Borough of Hammersmith and

Fulham, but they also take them rowing on the whole six-mile boat race course from Putney to Chiswick. Rowing is kind of offered like a PE session to the kids. That equates to just over 1,000 state school children. Each and every school that takes part has their own rowing kit, which you only tend to see in the likes of Eton and Cambridge, which once again helps to break down barriers of perception in society.

Their whole remit is about young people in the Borough of Hammersmith and Fulham, using rowing to enable them to find their potential, whatever that might be. To learn some new skills, to develop confidence and to make sure they're doing something constructive in the school holidays when maybe they would otherwise be sat at home.

I'd first met Imogen Walsh in 2012 through rowing, when I got released and she was still an international competitor. Then here I am now about to cross paths with her again, but on something far more important. Here's a little bit of context of Imogen's journey to Fulham Reach and eventually our paths crossing. Imogen had no aspirations of being a champion of any sort when she joined a rowing club. She got involved because of the community side of things, then the performance stuff came second. It turns out she was a pretty good rower and Imogen went on to represent Team GB for five years and became a European and two-time world champion.

However, before that she worked in international development for a charity and it was kind of her intention to go back to the charity after retiring from rowing in 2016, due to not making the Rio Olympics. However, she wasn't sure exactly what she wanted to do. All she knew was, she wanted to still be involved in the sports industry somehow.

While coaching sport for a few years, Imogen started to learn more and more about the criminal justice system. From her experience of how rowing had allowed her to be part of community and gave her a sense of purpose, she knew that sport, rowing in particular, was something that could help a lot of people behind bars.

When she joined Fulham Reach Boat Club, she spoke to the CEO at the time, Steve O'Connor, about whether there was some scope to use rowing in the criminal justice system. I was really close with Steve and we were discussing a project of getting people rowing in prisons and there was a lot of momentum there to get people from the prison service to do stuff. I had this relationship that was already developed with Michele Glassup at Feltham, and I said to Steve, 'Let's see if we can get Fulham Reach Boat Club to twin up with Feltham.' Imogen then got the job at Fulham Reach and the natural thing was to connect them. I took Imogen into the prison so she could see how it operated and introduced her to Keith Potter and Michele, who explained about their emphasis on rehabilitation through sport. The three of them were all on the same page, and were so passionate that they went above and beyond their remit to make it work.

Michele and Keith did everything they could to take Boats Not Bars into the prison and, from that, Imogen did the first pilot project in Feltham Young Offenders Institute (YOI) in spring 2019. The pilot went well and then from October 2019 they started doing it properly. At the beginning, it started off at Feltham YOI and we got six rowing machines, and Imogen would go in and deliver rowing sessions. However, some of these prisoners, while on licence, were then able to go to Fulham Reach Boat Club and do a rowing session on the water.

It took a little while to get going, and just as it was getting up to full steam, Covid happened in March 2020 and everything collapsed. They'd only been running for six months and, due to the pandemic, prisons took a very, very long time to reopen; a lot longer than the other communities outside.

Thankfully, by about the autumn of 2023 it was up and running again and in that time some prisons started to really enjoy the model of day release and taking prisoners out on to the river and meeting new people and getting used to the environments, which is something that stopped during Covid.

Other prisons have now come on board and the basics are mainly the same. Fulham Reach run an indoor rowing course and they invite everybody to come and connect with them when they're released. They may not want to touch a rowing boat or a rowing machine ever again, which is absolutely fine, but Fulham Reach just want to let them know they are there to help them with anything. Some prisoners transfer their skill of being able to row and others will want to teach prisoners how to row and get their coaching certificates. Very few will want to be rowing coaches, but the ability to stand up in front of a group of people and deliver a rowing session is a really valuable skill when it comes to things like job interviews. It helps with confidence of articulating the knowledge you have. That's really valid.

Some prisoner sessions that Fulham Reach host have psychologists in attendance at the prisons, within a gym setting, which is certainly better than, say, a healthcare consultation room. Getting people into the gym is key, because they feel at home and maybe let their guard down a little bit and you can start to talk about maybe what they were worried or anxious about or how their thoughts, feelings and behaviours connect, and understanding that maybe when they are nervous about something, it comes across as aggression, because they put their walls up and become really defensive. That then triggers to some kind of tension, which then potentially leads to a violent episode. Understanding themselves a bit more and how others may present themselves is perhaps not always an act of aggression; it might just be because they're nervous about something.

Thankfully, at the time of writing, Boats Not Bars is still going strong, with Imogen and her colleagues not only running the sessions in Feltham, but also delivering programmes to ten other prisons. That's progress.

Chapter 8

Keep On Running

'Prisoners bring a diverse range of people, backgrounds, ethnicities, fitness levels all together and the benefits of sport extend far beyond physical health and fitness. Mental health, emotional resilience, confidence, self-esteem, sense of purpose, sense of autonomy and, most importantly, a sense of connection to oneself and your environment. Being outside, being able to breath the air, see the sky and have a connection to other prisoners, who you may not normally converse with, or you may not see eye to eye with on the wing, but as parkrunner you are unified under a banner. Then outside of the prison, they are connected to a global community of over 11 million registered parkrunners. They are part of a community of over 350,000 that take part every weekend. You're connected to the world outside in a positive way.

'Whilst it's not a panacea and we know that those that are released from prison face many, many barriers to that positive rehabilitation into society, it does provide an opportunity to be integrated into a welcoming supportive, non-judgemental, positive community that could help reduce reoffending in that revolving door of entry into prison.'

—Chrissie Wellington OBE

I FIRST met Chrissie in 2017. As an athlete, she was one of the most incredible Ironman competitors that ever lived. Almost 20 years later, competitors are just about beating her times she set on shitty bikes, with crappy trainers and armed with little nutritional knowledge. She was a phenomenal athlete and was regarded in the sport as being the greatest of all time, winning four Ironman World Championships, almost on the bounce. When she retired from professional sport, she had her first challenge of filling that void.

Similar to Imogen, before becoming an athlete, Chrissie worked in international development and on retirement in 2012 wanted to combine her passion for physical activity with uplifting, empowering and motivating people. The same year, she met Paul Sinton-Hewitt, the founder of parkrun, and for a year she helped to set up junior parkrun. Her role evolved and she soon became Global Head of Health and Wellbeing, which involved developing interventions to engage those who would benefit most from parkrun. Those who are typically marginalised from the opportunity to be active, socially connected and healthy.

In 2017, Chrissie received an email from a physical education instructor at HMP Haverigg, saying they were interested in setting up the parkrun in their prison. The parkrun team took that enquiry from a seed to fruition and within six months had activated the first parkrun on the grounds of HMP Haverigg. Then later that same year, I contacted Tom Williams, who was Chief Operating Officer at parkrun at that time, and got on a call with him while driving on the A2 to Swanley. I said, 'It would be really amazing if you could get parkrun across a number of prisons,' and he said, 'We've thought about doing this before, but it's really difficult to get access to the prison service to be able to deliver this.' The MOJ got an email from one of the broadsheet newspapers asking them whether they could put parkruns on in prisons, and the MOJ were obviously mindful about any negative press. I said, 'I might be able to help.'

From that, Tom linked me up with Chrissie and we started a dialogue. She explained how she'd found it very difficult to engage with government and get time with them. I said to her, 'Leave it with me and I'll see if I can organise a meeting with Dr Phillip Lee. He's a massive advocate of getting sport into prisons and helping young offenders.' Phillip agreed to meet with us and I genuinely believe if it wasn't for him the doors to get parkrun into the UK prison system would never have opened.

I met Chrissie in person for the first time in a coffee shop opposite the MOJ and we had so many joint passions on many different levels that it took us very little time to really connect. Then the year after, when we presented at the MOJ, we included Chrissie and parkrun in Rosie Meek's Criminal Justice Reform report. Subsequently, parkrun has gone on to be active in the UK,

Ireland and Australia in prisons and YOIs, which Chrissie led on. What an achievement from her side.

The year we presented at the MOJ was the same year I met Michele Glassup, who does so much for the young people at HMP Feltham, along with Keith Potter, and it turned out she's also very good friends with Rosie Meek. Since being released, I've visited HMP Feltham quite a lot and one reason is because it marked a very important milestone on my timeline. I was in there as a prisoner for about four days, before being starred up to Cat A and moving me to HMP Woodhill, which was an adult prison.

They already had a very successful programme at HMP Feltham; then a couple of months after first meeting Michele, they invited me in with Mark Hunter, the GB rower, and Steve O'Connor, from Fulham Reach Boat Club. We came in for a visit and it took off from there in terms of me helping to set up a pilot of a Boats Not Bars. Then, in 2019, they set up HMP Feltham parkrun with Chrissie's help and they invited me to be part of that. I then started going back more frequently, which included doing the premier of *The Way of the Wildcard* video, which was a very entertaining day on several fronts.

Before the film was launched for general release, I asked the Red Bull team and Just So, the production company that made the film, if we could premier it at Feltham YOI. They agreed, and for me it was like a full-circle moment, going back to the first-ever prison I went to, when I was 18 years old, but now I was going back in to help others of a parallel age.

There was a lot of anticipation and nerves from the production team going in with me, because it was a really alien environment for them. We all met up outside the prison, then all went through checks, handed in all our smart devices, and I then noticed everyone getting more and more nervous. We went to the chapel where the screening was being held, and when we walked in, a prison officer who was there to escort the 90 or so prisoners who were going to watch the film got talking to me. He was very old school and I would guess had been in the system for maybe 25 or 30 years, and he started talking to me about the prisoners. I kind of got the impression he didn't think they had the ability to change. He was talking to me, not knowing that these prisoners were here for me and the content of the documentary, otherwise I'm sure he might have chosen his words more carefully.

I must admit, with that number of people, I did start to think, *This could end very badly*, because there were several gang problems in there at the time, although I didn't verbalise that to anyone with me. More and more prisoners started to arrive, and having been in prison for ten years, I can read a room and know when the atmosphere shifts. I was very alert to tension when new groups of people were walking in and the other prisoners were looking at them walking through the door; it set something off in me again that had been dormant. That hyper-alertness of being in that environment. Then another group of kids came in straight after and a fight broke out.

All the people I was with got very nervous because they weren't used to this. I said, 'It's all fine. The prison officers have this under control.' It looked more violent than it actually was as nobody was getting knocked out and it was more like handbags at dawn. Sometimes it's more the bravado. People walk in, and before they've even thrown a punch, they're screaming, because they want the attention, and the fight doesn't even happen, because the prison officers jump on them. To me, I knew it wasn't that serious, because normally if someone wants to hurt another person, they won't start screaming the moment they walk into a room; they would be quiet, go up to the person and then do what they want to do.

That fight got clamped down and then another group came in from another wing and, bang, it kicked off again. Panic buttons were being hit, sirens and bells were going off and, again, the guys I was with were pretty scared. The prison officers were telling them, 'Stay at the back and don't come over.' Then that lot were escorted out and another group came in and, bang, it happened again for the third time.

After the third incident, everyone was told to sit down. Keith Potter took the lead and got everyone to settle down. I then got up and started speaking to the kids and said, 'Listen. I was in your situation 15 years ago and I was in Feltham for a few days.' At that point they all started laughing, thinking my entire prison sentence was four days for maybe something like not paying a load of parking fines. Once they'd stopped laughing, I then mentioned

I got Cat A and was moved to Woodhill. The room went silent as their faces went serious.

It's a weird situation to be in those environments because there's a hierarchy within prison and those kids might not respect the sports side, but they can understand the meaning of Cat A. Once I'd told them my story, they respected me, which from my side means I have their attention, because to them, they would classify me as a serious person in the prison system. I then said, 'This film is about my life,' but I didn't really go into any detail, because I wanted the film to explain it. The moment they pressed play on the film, the room was totally silent and everyone was engaged in it, which was quite a powerful moment.

At the end of the film I explained the resilience that they all have, being locked in a cage for 23 hours a day and still getting up every single morning. I explained that if they could apply that mindset to something positive like I did, they would be able to stop committing crime and give themselves chances for a different life.

When we were walking out, the crew from Just So said, 'Wow. That was amazing. The violence, the atmosphere, the authenticity of the setting, followed by the prisoners watching the film and absorbing it, showed the influence it had.' The film brought tranquillity to chaos.

At the time of writing, HMP Feltham still do parkruns every Saturday morning. When the young people get released, they can keep that going, because it's a free initiative and they will find themselves in a really supportive network that sport generally brings, like teamwork and consistently training. All these disciplines that are very wholesome.

I've done quite a lot of parkruns in Feltham, and whenever I come back to the UK I try to do a run because I know how much it means to the kids. It's such a powerful experience when you're running around with them and especially when you're able to take in guests. We did a parkrun in Feltham around 2020 and I had four athletes that came in with me. Some of them worked for Goldman Sachs and found it a super-powerful experience, realising they weren't that dissimilar to the kids they were running around with. They got to grips with the lottery at birth and realised they had parents who supported them and had the resources to get them to university and support them through that and pursue a career in sport, which led them to become Olympic champions. These other kids didn't have these same advantages awarded to them.

It was great to bring in these athletes, because it also made them look at things differently. You can easily just look at kids and think they're just lazy, don't want to achieve anything in life and want shortcuts, but that's not the case. Here's an example. I brought in rowers Rob Willams and Mark Hunter. Mark's won a gold and silver at the Olympics and also gold at the World Championships, and Rob's won a silver at the Olympics. They came in, both high achievers in business now, and here they were talking to these young people, realising how lucky they are and how these young people didn't have a fair crack at the whip.

Michele Glassup took them on a tour of HMP Feltham after the parkrun and they had the chance to see a wing. When they saw a cell and that the windows didn't open, I remember one of them getting quite emotional and saying, 'How can someone survive for so many years in those conditions? How?'

Chapter 9

One Life

'For to be free is not merely to cast off one's chains, but to live in a way that respects and enhances the freedom of others.'

—**Nelson Mandela**

WHEN MARILYN, my social worker, retired around 2014, a young lady called Charlotte came in and became my new case manager. When she started working with me, she said, 'There's no point in you coming in every month. You can do quarters now. Check in with me every three months. Is that okay?' Obviously, I said, 'Yes!'

At the time, my life was so busy and during those half-hour sessions with Charlotte in Orpington, she'd ask, 'What have you been doing for the last quarter? How's life?' I'd say, 'Life's good. I went to the Ministry of Justice, I was with MP, Dr Phillip Lee, and spoke at this commission and I was also invited to the Tory Party conference to speak with him. I've also been to 10 Downing Street, I'm still working with Nike as a sponsored athlete and I've been meeting with a load of Olympians. I've also got a book out.' Charlotte looked at me with her eyes wide open like, *Bloody hell.* Sometimes I felt like I was lying to them, because it almost sounded far-fetched, so I used to bring in documentation to verify what I was up to.

My first probation officer, before Marilyn, was absolutely convinced I'd been given the wrong stretch. She said, 'I can't believe the sentence you are doing for the crime you've been convicted of. I've seen people who have been convicted of crimes far worse than you and they're serving sentences nothing remotely close to yours.' She even sent a letter to the judge that sentenced me and he came back and said, 'Yes. I did give him that sentence.' She couldn't believe it.

My life was so different at that point to perhaps many other ex-prisoners reporting into their probation officers. Even when I was meeting with Marilyn, I can remember doing rowing sessions on the water and then having to jump in the car and drive over to Orpington to meet her every few weeks and I'd still have my rowing gear on. It was the most bizarre situation. Charlotte acknowledged what I'd been doing with my time, and around 2018 she said, 'You shouldn't need to come here. It's such a waste of resources, because it's so clear that your life is different now, but this is the procedure.' I said, 'Where will this eventually end up going?' and she said, 'You'll probably get up to having to report just once a year, but at this moment that's not on the table.'

Up to this point I couldn't travel or live where I wanted to without permission. I had to stay within ten miles of my probation office, and then if I moved, my probation office would also be different. The risk with that was then trying to build up a rapport with new officers and getting their confidence. I'd built up such an amazing relationship with that office in Orpington with Marilyn and then Charlotte, and they were allowing me the opportunity to travel to the Netherlands to see Nike and let me live the dream as an athlete.

However, while I was meeting all these amazing people and doing all these competitions, this darkness was always hanging over me, because of my life licence. It was like I was living two different lives. To everyone else, though, they thought, *You're out of prison. You're free!* Well, actually, I wasn't. I couldn't do what I wanted. People used to ask me, 'Why don't you just move to Putney?' I'd say, 'Because, if I move to Putney, that means my probation office is going to be based in Wandsworth, and if I then started to ask this new officer, who didn't know me, "Can I take part in an Ironman competition in Germany?", they'd probably say no, because they didn't know me. To them I would have just been another life-sentence prisoner.'

When I was travelling somewhere, there was a formal process that had to go through the probation office to be signed off by Charlotte's boss, then her boss's boss had to sign it off, and there were conditions attached to that. I had to go and see them in the morning of the day I was leaving, then the day I got back, or the following morning, then I had to check in again with my probation office. If I didn't, they'd put out a warrant for my arrest to say I'd absconded abroad.

Marilyn and Charlotte really looked out for me. When I first met Marilyn, she asked, 'Are you in a relationship?' and I replied, 'No.' She said, 'I'll give you some advice. Whoever you get into a relationship with, make sure they are stable, because I do not want to be in a situation where I have to recall you, knowing you've done nothing wrong, but because someone said you'd done something wrong I would need to bring you back in. I have to do it all the time and then I'm duty bound to record the incident, because there's been an accusation made.' Between that and the travel and living restrictions, on occasions it was like walking across a field of eggshells, but Marilyn and Charlotte made the process the smoothest it could be.

I'll be honest, it wasn't easy. A mate of mine had a stag do in Paris at the end of the Tour de France on the last day, but I couldn't go because of my licence conditions. Then my friends at the rowing club would go on holiday and invite me, but again I couldn't go. All these sorts of things, I couldn't do spontaneously. Then even when I did fill out all the paperwork for an event, say, four months into the future, sometimes they'd fuck up the paperwork and I couldn't travel.

Here's another example. I trained for nine months for Ironman Hamburg in Germany, then the week before I phoned up the office and said, 'Can you send me the licence, please?' They said, 'We thought it was the following month.' I said, 'No. It's next week.' They couldn't do it. I'd trained all that time for that one event, was in amazing shape, but that's how this was. I just had to accept that my life was going to be like that forever and there would be no other options on the table. I was being quite stoic about it. There was no point in getting resentful or hateful against the system, because I didn't want to be like that. I put myself into that situation to get that sentence and empowered them to do that to me, so I had to accept the repercussions of that.

Then one day, my phone rings. Charlotte was saved under 'Probation Officer' on my phone and I noticed there had already been a missed call. Normally, when they phone you outside of your meeting dates, there's something wrong. I called her back. 'Hi, Charlotte. Is everything okay?' She said, 'I've got something to tell you and I don't fully know what this means, but we've had notification that your life licence is going to be taken away.' I replied, 'Right.' Then I said, a bit confused, 'Er … What does that actually mean?' She said, 'I genuinely don't know and neither does anyone in the office, because we've never dealt with this before. You're going to have to come into the office in the next four weeks and I'll give you a date to sign some paperwork, and at that point we'll know what you can and can't do.' I kind of shrugged and said, 'Okay,' because I didn't want to jump to any conclusions.

A few weeks later, on 21 March 2019, I went to see Charlotte and she walked me through to a back room where we used to have our meetings. On the table was this piece of paper. I sat down, signed the piece of paper and Charlotte said, 'You can now do what you want.' I replied, 'Anything?' She said, 'Yeah.'

Signing that piece of paper and walking out that probation office gave me this overwhelming sense of elation and relief. A darkness had been hanging over me and I didn't realise how much it hung over me until it wasn't there anymore. It was like I had the freedom I had when I was a kid and could do what I wanted, when I wanted. Once I'd come to terms with what had happened, I realised, *You are actually free to do what you want. You are not just free, but you have freedom.* We hugged, I walked out the door and then started to process what had just happened.

Obviously, I was ecstatic, but also a little bit suspicious, as I had no idea how or why the decision had come about in the background. I had a gut feeling it would have taken someone at a top level to have signed it off, and that turned out to be correct. Sajid Javid, then the UK's Home Secretary, lifted my life sentence conditions in recognition of my positive transformation. At this moment I was a bit shell-shocked, had some reservations and loads of questions, but it all sounded very promising. I was now thinking, *Where shall I live?*

This was the first time in a very, very long time that I was able to travel without asking anyone or needing to report into any probation officers. At the earliest opportunity, I got a flat with my mate and we lived across the road from the London Rowing Club in Putney. My whole life changed so much, but to everyone else looking in, they wouldn't have seen much of a difference. However, for me, I'd just entered a new chapter of my life. I had this sensation of appreciating the beauty of freedom, doing what

I wanted, when I wanted. I'd spent ten years in prison and it was the most free I'd felt since 2004 when I had that gap in between my two sentences. I was so unbelievably determined to make sure my future was not only positive for myself, but helpful and influential to as many people as I could help on this new journey I was about to embark on.

Chapter 10

New Ways of Living

'Intelligence is the ability to adapt to change.'

—Stephen Hawking

WHEN I was little, I used to love watching Michael Palin's, *Around the World in 80 Days* on BBC on a Sunday. There was one episode in particular where he was on a cargo ship, going across the equator, and he had all these rituals with the captain, and I thought, *I want to travel and visit different parts of the world.*

As far as my sister and mum go, their outlook on travelling and exploring was polar opposite. My sister was backpacking at 18 and was travelling all over the world for six or seven months at a time. As a kid, I have fond memories of receiving postcards from her, from all these different amazing places, and I used to stick them up on the wall. My mum, however, is not like that. She's like a homing pigeon and has spent her entire life in or around Crystal Palace and now Chislehurst. Her orbit is a trip to Sainsbury's or the Chislehurst parade of shops.

I do have to give some credit to Billy Tobin for an element of inspiration to travel. He used to have an apartment on Les

Champs-Elysées and always used to talk to me about France, Barbados, Jamaica and all these stories of him being out in the US with my sister. It's only now I realise that these stories must have had an impact on me, telling me, 'There's a big world out there and I want a bit of that as well.' However, when I got to my late teens, I had so much hatred towards the system and the government that it was almost as if I felt Britain was not my home. Admittedly, a big part of that was because I'd inflicted situations on myself, which resulted in me going to prison! I lost the best of my teenage years and my 20s behind bars, and the only time I felt alive was when I was in Spain or the Netherlands. So, I kind of saw the UK as prison in my mind. So, when I got released I had the opportunity to have a proper fresh start and move forward with my life, but in surroundings that were right for me. I knew there was more out there than where I grew up and I didn't want to accept that living in Crystal Palace for the rest of my life was where I would be.

Moving to the Alps involved a lot of life adjustments and making new choices. Some were quite obvious, like not having to report into probation officers, being surrounded by mountains, but other things kind of evolved over time.

I've always liked animals but never grew up with nature and was never exposed to animals in the outdoor world. The closest was probably a few dogs at Crystal Palace park. When I came to Alpe d'Huez after restrictions got lifted a bit after the first Covid lockdown, I knew this is where I wanted to live for the rest of my life. It would be a big move on a number of levels, especially as I would be all on my own, with no friends or family out there.

In the first few months, I was exploring the area, and in the evenings I would go to the top of the mountain to watch the sunset. I didn't realise it at the beginning, but there was this big equestrian centre, and in this field were these absolutely beautiful muscular horses with shiny coats. One evening, as I was going up, I went to the fence and they came over. I was giving them some grass and patting them, then the next night I stopped off at the supermarket, got them some carrots and apples and started feeding them regularly.

This became a routine most nights, and one night something clicked in my head. Maybe it was a build-up of things I'd been observing, like watching the sheep and cows in lorries with their noses poking out of the bars, going off to slaughter, and it made me feel really uneasy and uncomfortable. It reminded me of being in a prison van. This one night it was like a realisation of my own hypocrisy that I would eat a chicken or a fish, but I liked dogs and cats, and found myself thinking, *Why do you have an affection for one group of animals, but not others?* Also, being around these animals in the mountains, I started to realise they sensed me and had emotions, just like human beings. Just like that, I became vegan.

Like with everything, I went all in. No eggs, no milk, no honey. Nothing that is a product of animals or is in any way an exploitation of them. It was a big shift for me, because before that point I'd never heard of veganism and would have had no interest. Although I was never a massive meat eater, I used to eat chicken and fish, and just like that I switched it all off. Being in prison all those years taught me that discipline. Having that ability to live off porridge, peanut butter, nuts and fruit, because I refused to eat the shit prison food.

However, prison surroundings also made me underappreciate food. For me, food was just fuel, but that came with its own question marks now. I burn a minimum of 3,000 calories on a normal day and up to about 8,000 on race day, so I was now thinking, *Will the change to vegan affect my athletic performance?* My response to myself was, *I don't give a fuck if it doe*s. My principles and morals were more important based on the judgement I'd made on that night with the horses. For me, it was more about the discipline of not eating animal-based products again and not being a hypocrite to myself. That said, I get all my bloods taken regularly, have my heart, liver and kidneys checked, and I'm absolutely fine. Six years after turning vegan, the doctors are impressed with my physical state and I have a resting heartbeat of around 36.

Even though I push my body, I really look after it. I don't deprive myself of calories, because I'm very aware of what can happen to your body when you under-fuel, especially as an endurance athlete. You can overtrain and develop energy deficiencies, pick up fractures and tear muscles but, due to my calorie intake, at the time of writing as a 40-something-year-old, I don't feel any different to what I did in my 20s.

As I started to settle in Alpe d'Huez, I'd be hiking in these mountains for hours, then days and you're in your own world, not seeing any humans and you're thinking again, *What's life all about?* I'd then think about the journey that brought me to this place. Chasing money and how destructive that was for me and how I'd ruined other people's lives that I loved and cared for as a kid. You have to have that awareness that you can't just completely disconnect, though, because you can become a hermit at the top of a mountain before you know it. In fact, there's people that live near me who I didn't even know lived here, and I'm talking about after living in Alpe d'Huez for five years. I've only seen them maybe once or twice.

I genuinely believed the next part of my life would include a lot more travelling. Although I'm an introverted character in some regards who enjoys his own solitude and space, I feel the urge to explore, meet people and experience new cultures. It all comes down to being able to put that all together and do something positive with it. But what, though?

Chapter 11

A Different Approach

'During Covid, he couldn't do a lot on site, but instead of looking at what he couldn't do, he looked at what he could do. He worked with us and donated a copy of his book to every single young person in custody, which was over 2,000 books. The books arrived and we distributed them. Off the back of that, we also did a book review competition and John chose the winner and got them Nike trainers.'

—Michele Glassup

ROTL (release on temporary licence) & Resettlement, HMP & YOI Feltham

WHEN THE UK Lockdown started on 23 March 2020, being at home wasn't a big deal for me, because I'd been in far worse situations of restriction and had learned to survive without creature comforts. However, I did appreciate that, for many other people, dealing with a lack of freedom was very challenging.

At the time, I was doing stuff for the Trussell Trust, dropping parcels of food to vulnerable people who couldn't go to the trust's foodbank site, due to not being able to mix with others in case they got the virus. I was also trying to be of as much service as I could and raised about ten grand cycling from John O'Groats to Land's End on my indoor training bike. I could have done it in three days easily, but the longer I was cycling the more donations were coming in. My mate said, 'Stretch it out as long as you can!' I ended up taking six days.

With HMP Feltham, I really appreciated that those young lads were locked up between 23 and a half and 24 hours a day and I wanted to do something where the kids could have access to my book. When I was in segregation, that's how I built my life, 365 days a year, reading books and exercising. I wanted them to read my story and think, *Okay. It might be difficult at the moment, but you can still turn this perceived negative situation into a positive, better yourself and move forward with your life. You don't have to see this as a pause, you can see it as a reset and a rebuild.*

I approached the publisher and asked how much it would cost for 2,500 copies of the book, because that's how many young people were incarcerated in the UK at that time. I then spoke to the prison industry people, and what was difficult then was getting the books distributed across the prison service. Michele led on that and put an amazing amount of work into it, while I got the books sent to HM Prison Service Branston, which was a central hub for the prison service. They then packaged the books up and distributed them among the young prisoners, so every young person would get a copy of my book delivered in an information pack to their cells. That's when we also decided to do the book review competition.

The young people's reviews were good and it was quite funny to read how critical some of them were of the book, saying things like, 'There should have been more action.' We then picked a winner and that prisoner got a set of Nike trainers, which I had sent to Feltham, and Michele gave them to the prisoner. Small things, but it helped to take the edge off a very tense global situation, which was magnified even more behind bars.

At the age of 17, I was up for nine counts of robbery while other kids my age were starting work or were in colleges. For many youngsters, the notoriety of being a criminal is an attraction, but by telling my story and explaining the power of sport, I wanted them to realise how easily their lives could become something amazing, instead of just chucking it away trying to be something they shouldn't. After giving those books away, I started to receive messages from the parents, thanking me. The reality is that it's hard to know how many people's lives you have perhaps helped or influenced, but you have to have faith that what you are sharing and teaching has a positive effect.

***

Early December 2020, in between the second and the third lockdowns in the UK, I brought a lovely lad called Precieux Noka out to the Alps. He was about 20 at the time. Precieux was at the Gloves Not Gunz charity with Marek, turned his life around through boxing as a teenager and became a national champion. I explained to Adam Ballard, who was head coach at Croydon ABC and a director of Gloves Not Gunz, that I was doing a training camp in Annecy, France, and asked if I could take Precieux away on the trip. Adam said, 'He hasn't got any money, mate.' I replied, 'I'll cover it.'

By coincidence, I was talking to Nike London at the time and mentioned about possibly taking this kid out to the Alps to do a training camp. They asked, 'What are you going to be doing out there?' and I said, 'I'm going to teach him how to ride a road bike.' Nike thought it was amazing and that I was trying to inspire the next generation of Londoners. They asked if they could send a film crew down to document this trip, and I said, 'Okay. Cool.' I then spoke to Cervelo, who was my bike sponsor at the time, and asked if they could give me a bike for him. They gave us this amazing top-of-the-range carbon bike.

I lived in Putney back then. My mate, Aidan, lived across the road and Precieux stayed at my place the night before. We left at 5am the morning after, got to Calais, then drove from Calais to Paris, spending the night in Paris before heading to Annecy. The idea of the night in Paris was to give Precieux a bit more experience of being abroad. I booked up the accommodation and, because of the traffic, we didn't get there until late at night. Before getting to the accommodation, we drove to the Eiffel Tower, which was all lit up with flashing lights, and that blew Precieux away. We took some pictures and had a nice moment as there were some kids playing street football and everyone was interacting with each other.

We then got back into the car and drove to this tiny studio apartment in Paris, where you could barely swing a cat. Me and Aidan had to share a double bed, which he wasn't too happy about, and we let Precieux sleep on the sofa. We were in this bed and it was like this romantic scene when I opened up the window and there was a full moon, and we cracked up. He said, laughing, 'I'm never fucking letting you book anything again!'

We set off the next morning and we were in comms with the Nike film crew, because they wanted to get these shots of when our car was driving into Annecy, with them driving behind us filming. Well, it took us fucking ages because they didn't know where we were and we didn't know where they were. After an hour we eventually found them and they got these shots of us driving into the mountains until we got to our destination.

There were about five film crews and it was very Nike. Very professional. They're thinking Nike athlete, training camp, Alps. In their heads they're thinking a little shot of me getting out the car and getting my bike out, then Precieux's, spinning the wheels and making sure everything is working. Then they said, 'We'll follow you walking into your apartment, and we want that moment of Precieux's eyes lighting up as we walk into the apartment.' I said, 'That's absolutely fine,' but I was thinking, *It ain't gonna be the Hollywood scene you're expecting.*

They got all the cameras set up and we went round into the car park to walk up to the apartment. The cameraman was walking behind us and then we opened up the door. As we went to walk in, because the apartment was so small, we suddenly all had to stop. The guy behind the camera then said, 'Er … Yeah. Sooooo, we won't film this bit.'

Next morning they did a bit more filming, then we took Precieux out to the pontoon near where we were staying, just next to the mountains, which was beautiful. Then came the time to teach him how to ride a road bike. This was a top-of-the-range bike worth about 15 grand, but from his side it was all new and probably a bit daunting. He'd never been on a carbon fibre bike, never worn cleats and never used an electric gear shift. I ended up spending an hour with him, holding him up, explaining to him how to lock his foot in and out of the cleat and that, once it's in, it's locked into the pedal. I then explained how the electric gear shifters worked.

The only concern I then had was, *Can he ride up the Semnoz?*, which is a really famous climb on the Tour de France, with an average gradient of seven per cent. As I stood next to Precieux, I said, 'Tomorrow, this is what you'll be conquering.' He looked at the mountains and nodded. I then said, 'I've seen Olympic athletes getting off their bikes and pushing them up this mountain.' He said, 'This is something completely new to me, but I'm ready to be pushed mentally.'

We cut the first climb out to get to the bottom of the Semnoz, which still left a monster of a climb of about 13 or 14km, up to about 1,700m. The film crew was in the car tracking us and, just remember, Precieux has never ridden a road bike, full stop, and I was next to him, coaching him up, trying to use terminology that he could relate to in order to motivate him, such as, 'You're in the 11th round,' and when he was starting to say, 'It's too much, I can't breathe,' I'd say, 'You're in the championship rounds. Just keep turning your legs, one stroke after the other. You're in the championship rounds.' He started screaming, 'I can do it, I can do it!' As he was starting to struggle for the last bit, I said, 'Take in the scenery, mate. It makes it all worth it. You're in the clouds now. Give me everything you've got now.' He shouted out, 'Pain is temporary. Quitting lasts forever.'

We got to the top of this mountain and he said, 'I can't feel my legs. That's the hardest thing I've ever done,' and I hugged him. I said, 'You did amazing. I'm so proud of you. I can't believe you've just managed to get up that.' Considering he'd never ridden a road bike before, he actually got up there pretty quickly. Standing there with Precieux and Aidan was such a powerful moment and it made me think about trying to create a cycling Alpine Run Project one day. Who knows? The bike brought me to the mountains and allowed me to create Alpine Run (more about that soon), which in turn allowed me to bring Precieux to the mountains. If I could give more kids the experience of road riding, that would be amazing. The main problem is the danger. With Precieux, we were able to do it in a very controlled manner because, once he'd ridden up to the top, I made sure the camera crew put him and the bike in the car and then drove down, because I wouldn't feel comfortable with him descending 25km off the top of a mountain pass doing 70 or 80kph on a bike on mountain roads.

That trip for Precieux was a life-changing experience. He went back to London and became a more amazing youth leader in the boxing club than he already was and he became a mentor for all the other young kids at the centre in Norwood, Crystal Palace. I'm very proud of him.

***

A couple of weeks later, I decided to go to Girona in northern Spain to train for three weeks. It was a five-hour drive from Alpe d'Huez, and when I crossed the Spanish border, the road signs changed and that triggered something in me. I thought, *The last time you were in this country was 2004.* When I left Spain back then, I was a completely different human being. I was leaving to go to the UK as an armed robber and a guy that was selling drugs, plus I thought I was only going to be over for a week. Well, I got arrested and it took 16 years to come back for this cycling training camp. It was such a powerful feeling. If you'd have said to me all those years back, 'John, you won't be coming back for almost two decades, but, when you do, you'll be a sponsored athlete,' I wouldn't have believed you. Yet, here I was.

It was a bit surreal to be cycling during the pandemic, because of the regional restrictions, but thankfully I had a special pass as an athlete, which allowed me to cycle outside the designated 10km radius during lockdown. It was quite funny, though, because people were tearing the arse out of it, proper making fun of the system and getting passes left, right and centre. You had people's dad's cycling with massive pot bellies, riding these really expensive bikes, pretending to be professional athletes, and if the police stopped anyone, all you had to do was show your pass. However, there were also some elite athletes out there. One day, I was out with James Mitchell, who did the front cover photo of my first book, and we went to go up the Mare de Déu del Mont, which translates as Mother of God of the Mountain, to do some photos. As we were driving up, we saw Ironman world champion Jan Frodeno riding up with a group of cyclists, and everyone in that group was a world champion in their sport. Then coincidentally, a little while after, we met him at the top of the mountain and had a nice chat. Lovely bloke.

Shortly after getting back from Girona, I officially moved to Alpe d'Huez, which again was a bit surreal. The first time I'd ever been to the mountains was in 2014, when I was given permission to train at Lake Annecy in the French Alps. Then in 2018 I went to Alpe d'Huez and I fell in love with the scale of the mountains. That was also my introduction to training at altitude above 3,000 metres. The easiest way to describe it is that you feel that you're not fit and starting from zero again. First thing I noticed was that my heart rate was through the roof and the effort was far more laboured because there's less oxygen available to breathe in.

However, when you get completely acclimatised to the altitude and go back down to sea level, you feel bomb-proof. Cycling at 2,000 metres in Alp d'Huez and running as high as 3,350 metres changed my fitness dramatically. When I came back to London and went out on my bike, I started tapping the heart-rate monitor thinking it was broken, because it was so low for the effort. More than anything, Alpe d'Huez profoundly changed my life and gave me the space to take a good look at myself, but for the first time in my life I felt like I was at home somewhere, compared to my turbulent and transient life in crime, where I never felt settled.

One of my first mates to come over and visit me in my new digs was James 'Monty' Montague. Here's a bit more about Monty. He was working in Portland, Oregon at Nike headquarters in basketball at the time; then he got a phone call to work in the football side of things, moved back to London and became the youngest-ever GM at Nike Football.

In 2017, I'd been in to speak to some Nike employees, and Monty's colleague Tom said to him, 'You've just missed one of the most amazing life story speeches I've ever heard. This eclipses so many of the other big names we've had speaking. It's so different and inspiring.' Monty then went through Dan Smith and Dan sent me a message: 'John. This is very unusual, but the new GM of Nike Football wants to have a chat with you. Would you like to meet with him?' I said, 'Yeah. No problem.'

Monty then contacted me directly and was honest and said, 'I missed your talk. Is there any chance we can meet?' I said, 'Of course.' I went up to his office and we had a chat for about three hours and clicked from the get-go. It also turned out he was good friends with Chris Edmends and Toby Hunter, which is no surprise, as they're all top lads.

Then, shortly after I'd moved to Alpe d'Huez, Monty was a bit stressed at work and at home, because he had a newborn baby, and his missus said, 'Why don't you go and see John in the mountains?' He contacted me and I said, 'Get out here, mate!'

Monty turned up at Alpe d'Huez and had no idea what to expect. He'd been skiing in the mountains, but he'd never been to a skiing resort in the summertime. He met me and my friend, Lisa Melvin, who was a triathlete, and I said all upbeat, 'We've got you a bike for tomorrow! No expectations, but we'll just go out for a little ride, just to show you the town.' That's how we pitched it to him, not realising he hadn't been on a bike since he was about 12 years old.

The next morning, I said to Monty, 'You might want to put some energy gels in your back pocket,' and he was like, 'I thought it was a gentle bike ride?' We descended from Alpe d'Huez, which was about a couple of thousand metres and, at this moment, he was thinking, *This is one of the best moments of my life. I'm here with McAvoy and Lisa and we're descending down this beautiful mountain in France*, which required no effort, because it was all downhill. Then we got to the valley and it suddenly dawned on him that he'd need to pedal back up. I said, 'You can get the bus if you want,' and you could see the relief in his face. Then I said, 'But you probably don't want to do that, I'm guessing?' Monty was thinking, *For fuck sake!*, but instead he said, 'Yeah, yeah. I'm up for that,' making out he was all enthusiastic for the bike ride.

Monty spent the next three hours at the back of Lisa's wheel, while I kept going up, disappearing and then coming back to help him. At one point, I was riding next to him and was pedalling to help push him up, like a ride assist. That was his induction into riding a bike in the mountains.

A good cyclist would do it in about 60–90 minutes, but it took Monty over three hours, which turned into one of his greatest achievements. From that moment, he not only got the cycling bug, but got himself into great shape. He came back two years later and did it in an hour and ten minutes, which I was very proud of. At the time of writing, Monty's not worked for Nike for about five years and we're still really good friends, which just goes to show, my relationships with people are not just transactional.

In the same way Monty made adjustments, I also made a few changes in my own exercise routine. I didn't consciously stop doing Ironman, but the last one I did was in 2019 and then, due to a mixture of events with Covid and moving to the Alps, I just decided I loved riding my bike and running in the mountains instead of the swimming side of things. That was that. Little did I know that I'd be adjusting my outlook on running in the not too distant future.

***

While still in the middle of the pandemic, in 2021, a production company at the BBC contacted me and said, 'Would you be interested in coming on a TV show? We can't tell you who will be hosting it, but the person is a famous actor.' I said, 'You need to give me some more context about what the show is about and what you want me to do.' They sent back an email saying, 'It's called *Fight School*, and it's named after the person hosting the show. Within it, we take a group of young people on this journey of learning how to box and we get them to do different challenges each week. It's all about discipline and life skills and they will be training to take part in a boxing match at the York Hall in Bethnal Green. We would like you to be a part of one of the episodes, with you taking them rowing and telling them about your story.' I said, 'I'm interested, but I would need to know who the person is that's doing the show,' because there's certain people I wouldn't want to work with, regardless of who they were. They came back and asked if I'd sign a non-disclosure agreement, and I said yes. I signed it and they came back and said, 'It's Idris Elba.'

It went a bit quiet and then they came back to me and said, 'It's been greenlit by the BBC to come out in 2022. Can we jump on a call with you?' We spoke about their expectations of me and I was then giving them ideas of where we could shoot the episode where I'd be featured. I said that I was an ambassador for Fulham Reach Boat Club in Hammersmith and we could potentially do it there. We then spoke about how the episode would pan out and they wanted me to be on it in the capacity of a coach, talking to them about rowing and then in the afternoon they wanted me there to tell the kids about my backstory. So, when I first turned up, they thought I was just a rowing coach.

I turned up at Fulham Reach Boat Club and there were five or six massive trucks, cameramen, make-up artists, you name it. It was the biggest TV thing I'd ever done. Then the producer and director said, 'Errrrr, Idris isn't coming today. He's sick. The episode is yours.' I said, 'Mine to do what? What do you want me to do?'

The kids turned up and we took them into the ergo area of the club and told them what the morning was going to look like. One of the girls had quite an angry expression on her face and I pulled her aside and said, 'Are you okay?' She replied, 'I don't want to do this. I've already told everyone I don't want to be in water.' I said, 'How come?' She said, 'My little brother nearly drowned in a kayak.' I said, 'I give you my word, nobody is going to force you to row on that water. All I'm going to ask from you is that when we do the stuff on the rowing machines, just give that your best. Then when we go out in the afternoon, you don't need to take part in the races on the Thames.' I managed to get a load of anxiety away from her and she started smiling as she was rowing on the machine. We all started having a bit of a laugh and there was loads of banter and encouragement going around within the group, because it was all new for them.

We then had lunch and I found it a bit of a weird experience, if I'm honest. These kids were all living in a nice house near St John's Wood and it was a bit like *Big Brother* as cameramen and crew were around just sitting there. The kids, who were mainly teenagers, were talking to them like parents.

There was one young lad called Zeb, who I instantly bonded with. A genuinely lovely kid, but I could tell he was also quite troubled within himself. He revealed to me that he watched his best friend get stabbed to death and he got charged with the murder, because the police thought it was him, when it wasn't. Eventually he got out, but he was suffering from paranoia and PTSD. The last sparring session before his fight at Bethnal Green he punched the coach because of a misunderstanding with a mouthguard, which he claimed was someone else's and had blood in it. He then ended up being barred from fighting on television and the BBC had to pull him out of the event. Idris asked me what I thought about Zeb being pulled, and I said, 'Well. He's got some issues, but you can't give up on him, because that's what everyone's ever done. You have to help him. He needs to be supported. That's what this project is about, right? Giving these kids opportunities, but also supporting and helping them. Is there things you could do for Zeb? Open up some doors of opportunity?'

The problem for me was what happened afterwards. There was nothing there to bind me and Idris Elba together, because I did that episode on my own, so they then needed to do another filming day with me and him, where I went over to a coffee shop in Bethnal Green, East London, where it was all staged with me and him sitting there. I mean it in the nicest way, but I could tell he'd probably only had a very small briefing about my story, which meant I had to bring him up to speed as to why I'd been approached. When I told him my story, he said, 'They should make a film about your life.' Stranger things have happened …

I left and ended up hooking Zeb up with a mate of mine called Joe, who's a property developer. He took him under his wing and started helping him. Fundamentally, what the show was trying to achieve was great, but the sad part is that if you were to ask anyone involved in that programme, 'Where are these kids now?', nobody would have a clue. There were no real life-changing opportunities off the back of that show and there was a lack of consistency of being in that person's life after and helping to open doors for them. Yes, it won't work for all the kids, but you have to try, because a few will have their lives changed.

One project that did come to full fruition by the end of lockdown in summer 2022 was Open Doors. I already mentioned earlier about how this started back in 2017–18 at government level, but on 6 June 2022 I was so happy to post this on Instagram: 'Today an initiative that I spearheaded with Nike and UKActive has launched the Open Doors UKActive blueprint. A new guide which has the potential to unlock the UK's school sport facilities, giving every child and young person access to activities and healthy food outside of school hours … It represents a universal model for unlocking the sports facilities on the doorstep of every community, providing essential support for children and young people's physical, mental and social wellbeing – particularly for those from low-income households.'

The legacy from Open Doors was twofold. Firstly, it was recognised in the government's 2023 strategy as a great example of projects that work, but also it led to wider projects, which the government funded, called Opening School Facilities, which ran from 2022–2025. Although I wasn't involved in that, it was great to see how that initial seed evolved and how these facilities had been offered to hundreds of thousands of kids who went through the Open Doors project.

One participant, who was a young girl taking part in the Open Doors programme (source: ukactive) said, 'I really wanted to do something in the holidays as normally I sit in my room on TikTok.'

One thing that did help many people during lockdown was technology. However, technology is like a wild animal that needs to be tamed. If you let it overtake your life, you are not in control, and unfortunately that's what happens to so many of the younger generation with social media. However, if it wasn't for technology, especially during lockdown, so many amazing events wouldn't have taken place, as I was about to find out.

'When I joined my local youth club, they asked, "Tell us a fun fact about you.' I said, 'When I'm older I want to live in the mountains." Then when the possibility to take part in the 2023 Alpine Run Project came up, they said, "This looks amazing and something we think you would be interested in, because of your love for mountains and the outdoors."

'It kind of went from there ...

'When I applied, I had no expectations. I really wasn›t expecting anything, especially with no prior running experience, but I at least wanted to do my part and try. I'm someone who really wants to try new things, push myself out my comfort zone and go for every opportunity. The small chance that I could potentially get on to it really excited me and planted a seed in my mind of the possibility – what if it did happen?

'I was shocked when I found out I had got it; a dream come true – the chance to finally visit the mountains!

'Everything happened so fast. From the initial interview, it was only a week later that all the selected participants were invited on to a call where John broke the good news that we had been accepted on to the project and would be travelling to London to the Nike HQ the following week!

'I was a bit nervous doing the train ride from Newcastle to London, because I'd never travelled that far alone before and it involved changing trains, which made me wonder if I'd even make it in one piece to London! Joining the project had a massive impact on my life in terms of travel, experiencing new countries and seeing what our beautiful world has to offer.

'As for actually seeing the mountains, nobody can prepare you for something that big, that incredible. When we first got to the Alps, it was really misty and foggy, so we couldn't actually see the mountains properly. Then as the days went on, the landscape began clearing up day by day and it was the constant "wow," of seeing more of it.

'On race day, when we got to Courmayeur, in Italy, everything totally cleared and the landscape opened up. There was a really special moment where I got to the highest point of my race and there was this clearing in the woods, I gasped. I had a moment of "Wooooow." I could see the whole mountain range, which was breathtaking. Then when you get to Chamonix and cross the line for the UTMB, that's also something that you need to experience in person, because hearing about it is completely different. The energy, the noise, the hype, the emotions.

'In terms of the mountains, if I had seen them on my own, I don't think it would have been as special. Being on this journey with the others, the build-up for six months, training so hard together as a team and finally the end goal, being able to experience that first time of seeing the mountains together made it something else.

'As a young devout Muslim girl from Newcastle, I would encourage young girls from any background to take part. Too often there's certain narratives created about Muslims through the media – assumptions of who we are and what we can and can't be – so much of which is simply not true.

'My faith is an integral part of my lifestyle, and what I love about Alpine Run Project is you don't lose your identity and you can still be who you want to be; I've been able to integrate into it while still being myself and staying true to my values. I am proud to express who I am; I wear my hijab and cover my hair, but I want to show that I deserve to be out here.

'In fact, trail running makes me feel connected to my faith – not separate. In Islam, there is an emphasis on reflecting on the world around us – on observing, pondering and recognising the signs within creation. Trail running has given me a way to do that and being out on the trails has allowed me to discover new places and appreciate the beauty of God's Earth.

'For me, I haven't seen many young Muslim girls in this space, or taking part in events like UTMB. Now, seeing them take part through the Alpine Run Project means a lot to me. Being able to share my journey, offer training advice and reassure others that they belong here too feels important. If I can do it, you can too. And no one should ever feel like they have to leave their identity behind to prove that.

'When you get to grips with John's past, you can easily think, "He's going to be a really chaotic person," but when you meet him in person, he has a calmness about him and when he speaks, we all get so much value of what he says. He's a very genuine person and everything he says comes from the heart and he really believes in the project and wants to make a positive impact. I'm really glad I've met him through ARP and I think he's super-cool – he's now absolutely living his best life in the mountains!!'

—Nimrah Sohail

Chapter 12

Tall Order

'I love working with John. He's got this really positive energy and it's really inspiring to see how much these kids have changed. It's really nice, because they have grown with him and, in the meantime, John's become a really good trail runner. He put his career slightly on hold to support the Alpine Run initiative.'

—Sabina Mollart Rogerson

I FIRST met Jasper Kain at an event in 2018 at The Gherkin in Central London, which we'd both been invited to, and here's how this all came about. I did a literature festival down in Wells, Somerset and the lady who was supposed to interview me got sick and was replaced by this lady called Marinda, who owned an agency. At the end of the Q&A, she said, 'I've got this event on Thursday at The Gherkin. Would you like to attend? It's got nothing to do with this stuff. I run this agency and it could be beneficial for you in sporting circles.' That's how I got invited and Jasper got invited through someone else.

The event was launching the release of a marketing report that talked about using technology in football to help advertisers and marketeers to change the way they delivered advertising in football stadiums. Things like the pitch would be like a screen. When players run, you could see a heat map through this technology, and when a goal was scored, the fans in the stadium could watch all this technology. The report also talked about how football needed to evolve with regards to changing times and fans. More and more kids now are mercenary. They follow a club, not a player, and they had all this data to prove that. All very interesting stuff.

The person who set up the event at The Gherkin said, 'You two need to sit next to each other,' basically because we were both passionate about helping young people. We swapped details and I went down to several youth sessions in south London for a charity Jasper was running at the time called Football Beyond Borders. We used to drive around and I would tell my story to the young people and I'd answer any questions from the kids. Sometimes we even had to play the game where certain schools didn't want me to meet the pupils because of my background, so Jasper used to organise some of these talks at youth centres, to bring the kids from the schools to the youth centres. Bear in mind, at the beginning, there were a lot of staff at schools that didn't believe I'd changed. They were worried about what sort of stuff I'd be saying to them and the influence it could have, which I totally get, but it was important for me to get across that I had genuinely changed and, most importantly, how I'd gone through that transformation.

Me and Jasper kept in touch and, in 2019, when I moved to Alpe d'Huez, we kind of vowed that we would bring out some young people to experience the mountains. Then Covid hit and that messed everyone's plans up.

Fast forward to June 2022. My mate Chris Edmends is a keen cyclist and had been talking about wanting to come over for a while to do a ride. Finally, with the pandemic behind us, he made it over. On this particular morning, I said, 'We're going up the Col de la Croix de Fer today. What's your FTP [functional threshold power]?', which is the highest average power a cyclist can maintain for approximately one hour. He said, 'About 260.' An FTP is measured for an hour max, so I said, 'If we sit at 200, we'll be fine.'

We get going and Chris is basically doing his FTP, which meant in about an hour he was going to blow up big time. Halfway through, I'm just enjoying the scenery and had one hand placed on the handlebars while voice-noting, sending emails and answering calls with the other. In the meantime, Chris is trying to stick on my wheel, doing his max power. I came off the phone at one point and turned to Chris and said, 'Sorry about that, mate. It's one of the guys working on that film about my life. He was asking for some information about a car we'd used for a getaway and was completely wrong, so I just needed to get it sorted.'

I was chatting at normal speed, nice and composed and Chris could hardly speak. Then about three and a half hours into the ride, which was about 2km from the top of Alpe d'Huez,

Chris started to blow up and had to stop at a bus shelter for a Coke. I asked him, 'Have you eaten breakfast?' and he said, 'I had a croissant.' He expected to do a five-hour bike ride in the mountains fuelled on just one croissant!

About two hours later, we got back, and I said, 'Right then. In an hour, we'll go for a hike.' Chris said, 'Errr, great,' whereas what he was thinking was, *Fuck*. We hiked to the top of this mountain and we had a drone with us. We just sat there looking out over the mountains and it was an amazing moment. Chris said, 'John. There's a part of Nike's running strategy, which is "Runners Helping Runners", and that's ultimately what you do. We need to find a way to take this community work and turn it into a multiplier effect. You need to be able to go in to change the lives of few, but impact the lives of many.'

I then asked, 'How will it work?' We talked a lot about whether we could take one kid from each key city who had maybe never seen a mountain or travelled much in their lives. We then started talking about partners and how the project might look. Fundamentally, we wanted to get the kids out to Alpe d'Huez, show them the mountains and get them running. Little did we know this was going to be the start of something special.

You can have a great idea, but if it doesn't fit into a specific corporate strategy, it won't work. Chris helped to join a lot of the dots together and helped me understand how the business side worked, so when I was talking to them, it allowed me to talk to them in a language they understood. They'd then say,

'Okay, that plugs into what we are looking to do,' instead of just floating around.

At the time, Chris was working for Nike but looking after the JD Group, who didn't do much in running because they were seen as more of a lifestyle retailer. He explained that if I could get Nike UK sports marketing and Nike European running invested, then getting a retail partner like JD on board, who already had a core following, could help amplify the message through their network.

Chris left Alpe d'Huez the day after and headed back to the UK. He wasn't even back from the 90-minute plane journey home, but when he landed there was a five-minute voice message from myself asking, 'How can we get this moving?'

A few weeks after Chris left, in July 2022, I was racing my bike in the Tour de Mont Blanc, which is a 330km loop with 8,300 metres of elevation and goes through France, Switzerland and Italy. I was then going to do a couple of local races to where I live, but I decided from August to the rest of the summer that I was going to go in the mountains and go hiking instead.

***

When I got into endurance sport, the UTMB (Ultra Trail Mont Blanc) is something I always knew existed as it's considered to be the pinnacle of trail running; however, it wasn't an immediate priority for me when my life licence was lifted. But once I got settled in Alpe d'Huez, I got talking to my friend Ami, who does marketing for brand activations and stuff like that, and it came up in a conversation. I said, 'I'd love to do the UTMB,' and she replied, 'I know the PR team.' I said, 'Do you reckon they'd be able to let me enter and race?'

It's the biggest trail running race in the world, with 10,000 people from around the world competing. The best of the best turn up to race each other. It's like the World Cup of trail running and you've got different distances you can do, such as a 55km race, 100km race, 140km and then the pinnacle, which is the 171km race where the best go against the best, clocking up to 10km of elevation.

Ami linked me up with a lady called Sabina Mollart Rogerson, whose agency does the PR for the UTMB. I asked, 'Would it be possible for me to have a spot to do the MCC?' The MCC is the first race of the week on a Monday and it's for volunteers or locals that live in the vicinity of the postcode of that part of the Alps. It's a 40km trail race that starts in Martigny-Combe in Switzerland and finishes in Chamonix, France, with a little under 2,500 metres elevation gain.

I sent her a couple of links about myself and she emailed back and said, 'I watched the video and found it interesting. We'd like to give you a bib for the MCC.' I was absolutely buzzing. We got chatting and Sabina mentioned how my project fitted in well in terms of them trying to expand the UTMB's appeal to a wider audience and maybe not just trail runners.

I had six weeks to get ready for it, but I'd been riding my bike, so I was very cardiovascular fit. However, I wasn't trail running fit, which meant I wasn't going to be super-fast, but I knew I had the mental strength to get round. I now had to get out on the trails and get myself conditioned for this race, so started my training in Alpe d'Huez.

Two days before the race, I drove over to Chamonix on my own, booked an Airbnb and knew absolutely nobody in the region. When I booked my digs, I thought it was for me on my own, but when I turned up I didn't realise I was staying at this old 75-year-old Frenchman's house in Chamonix, with him and his wife. His name was Bernard and he and his wife were basically renting one of their rooms out. As I pulled up into his drive, he was waiting at the front door with a big smile and then when I got inside his wife was waiting.

Bernard and his wife were amazing. He'd grown up in Chamonix since he was a kid, had worked in the post office, was a mountain climber when he was younger and still hiked now. He had this poster on his wall that said, 'You only age when you stop doing the things you love doing.' He was telling me about how much Chamonix had changed over the years and how massive the UTMB was for the town. I developed a great relationship with him, even though he didn't understand what a vegan was. First morning I was there he had butter and milk on the table and I said, 'I'm really sorry, I can't. I'm vegan.' They made no fuss and the next morning his wife went up to the shop and found soya milk and got me vegan butter. They were so, so lovely.

There I am in Chamonix on my own, staying in this house and not knowing anyone in the local area, when Sabina invited me to a drinks gathering of all the runners of note that were taking part in the races, plus some documentary filmmakers. I had some good chats there, left a couple of hours later and then put my head down for some sleep for the race the day after.

On the day of the race, I was absolutely motoring. I'd had a really good season on my bike, so I was so aerobically fit, especially on the flat or inclines. I was always a good Ironman runner and could run a sub-three-hour marathon in an Ironman; however, mountain running was still an unknown to me.

The first part of the race was uphill, covering over 1,000 metres of ascent in the first 7km, but because I had the leg power from cycling, at one point I was in the top 40 overall and everyone else was walking. I was like, *Fuck this. I'm going to run past them.* What I didn't realise was that there was a technique with trail running, and you didn't run the hills. You walked them really quick.

There I am running past loads of runners with my big quads and massive calf muscles, and as I pass this one guy, he says, 'You've got legs like a cyclist!' I did the first 7km, then it flattened off, then it was downhill and up. What starts to fuck your legs up is running off the mountains, because it's eccentric load, which meant my muscles were lengthening under tension. With the up and the flat, because I had cycling endurance, my legs were alright, but running off the mountains, my legs started to fatigue really badly because my muscles weren't used to working eccentrically because I hadn't done enough training in the mountains. As a result, I started to cramp up and felt a bit of shuddering in my quads.

When I got to the last big stretch downhill into Chamonix, I was running through this field and I was kind of running on my own, because ability spreads the competitors out. It's not like a conventional marathon. You could run for hours and not see someone in the same race, even though there are thousands of you competing. As I was running into Chamonix, Mont Blanc was on my left and it was an unbelievable sight, which had a profound effect on me. The hairs on my neck stood up and I had this massive wave of endorphins as if I was listening to my favourite music. I felt like I was in complete flow state and I had the most euphoric experience of my body feeling at one with the mountain and nature. The grass looked so vibrant, the sky was bright blue and when I crossed the line in Chamonix town centre, even though I had nobody there to support me, I thought, *That's the most amazing experience I've ever had in my life*. The purity of it, without any fanfare. That brought me back to the conversation I'd had with Chris, and I thought again, *How can I create this project to open up this beautiful place to kids who might not otherwise experience this?*

I was buzzing after the race and decided to go to see Sabina at La Folie Douce hotel in Chamonix, where the UTMB was based. I needed to have a chat with her before going to Nike to present my project idea, to make sure I could get bib entries for the race, which is the most difficult part, because the UTMB is the most sought-after trail race in the world. I spoke to her about my idea, but obviously she was up to her ears because the scale of the event is mind-boggling. I'd raced on the Monday and there were still four full days of races to go. She said, 'Let me get this event out of the way and then I'll try and help as much as I can.' She certainly stuck to her word.

The thing with the 171km UTMB is that the scale and level of difficulty means competitors have to prove they are good enough to race, and need to qualify. However, the other races are open to the general public, but it's always oversubscribed. The problem with my project was, and is always going to be, that due to the recruitment process we're only going to know shortly before the race who our kids are. We're talking around the end of June, early July, for an August race, whereas the bib entries have gone in January.

A couple of days after the UTMB dust had settled, we started the dialogue again and I explained about the work I'd been doing with Jasper and Youth Beyond Borders, and through me she got to know Jasper and his team quite well. With UTMB, there were certain things we were trying to develop in terms of youth and diversity and this project was a perfect fit from that perspective. I explained that there would be several training camps elsewhere, but ultimately the UTMB would be the big icing on the cake. Despite a very positive vibe, I still knew it was a tall order and must admit that when Sabina ringfenced the bibs for us, I was over the moon. Not only that, she also really encouraged us to use the UTMB as 'the' challenge in the summer. Sabina's been amazing in not only getting our foot in the door but keeping it in there for the long haul.

When I got home to Alpe d'Huez, I was thinking, *How am I going to do this?* I then thought, *I'm going to send a member of senior management an email.* I said, 'I've got an idea about trail running and I'd like to run it past you. Could you give me some time at HQ, please?' He replied, 'No problem.'

I knew I'd have to do a presentation at Hilversum and had a go at putting together a PowerPoint. Well, fucking hell, it was awful. This is where Toby Hunter really helped a lot. Helping to structure the presentation and rationale for such a project and relevant support required, equally driving the message within Nike on my behalf. I know my strengths and weaknesses and PowerPoint presentations or corporate politics is not a strength for me. Put me in front of a room of people and I can sell the dream, but I'm not the admin, techy person.

At this point, I kept referring to the idea as a project, or an initiative, but when getting together the pitch for Nike, that's when the birth of the title of the project came about, because it had to have an identity. It wasn't like we had focus groups to brainstorm the best name, it was literally me thinking, *So … it's in an Alpine setting … it's a run … and it's a project. Voilà – Alpine Run Project!*

I had a chat with Toby about the idea and he generously put some personal money towards the project, as did I, and that paid for me to bring out six kids from Football Beyond Borders, which Jasper Kain ran. Before Covid, me and Jasper had been talking about getting the kids out to the mountains and now we were out of lockdown we were about to make it reality. The weekend after I ran the MCC, it was possible for Jasper to drive a minibus from Manchester, then to London and out to see me. He took six young people on a crazy 16-hour drive and, when they arrived, I had an itinerary to open up the mountains to the young people.

We woke up early for sunrise and they didn't know what they were going to be doing. I had my friend Lisa Melvin helping me run it, and she got on a mountain bike and set off first up Alpe d'Huez; then me, the kids, a youth worker and Jasper met her at the top of the mountain. We were able to engage them in activities that made them a bit more present and gave them the essence of what the mountains were really about – that peace and tranquillity. We did a 5km trail run, which a couple of the kids struggled with massively, but we also did a range of other activities like wild swimming, hiking and white-water rafting. One memory that stuck with me from that trip is when one of the kids said he saw a cow. I said, 'You sure? You don't tend to see them on this terrain.' He pointed it out and it was a sheep. You have to remember, he'd never seen either before, so this was a learning curve on a number of levels.

That trip is where the Alpine Run was born. That was the first core group that ever came away to the mountain. It was such a powerful experience, but so simple. Sabina was instrumental in allowing me to develop a relationship with UTMB, and her team have been amazing. With that in place, I now had to pitch the idea to Nike. Hilversum, here I come.

At 10 Downing St with Lawrence Dallaglio, Professor Rosie Meek and Tanni Grey-Thompson, meeting Teresa May's policy team

At the EU – talking about the power of sport

At the United Nations with Toby Hunter's daughter, Gracie; talking to the international labour organisation

Breakaway cycling event at Oudenaarde Prison, with Big D

With Chris Edmends, formulating the backbone to the Alpine Run Project

David Davies putting Dr Phillip Lee through his paces at HMP Lowtham Grange

With David Dein discussing the Twinning Project

With Terry Williamson, Jasper, Monty at Chelsea FC

At Tottenham FC speaking to first team and academy players

With Precieux and Aidan O'Flaherty, on our cycling adventure

First ARP cohort in Alpe d'Huez

Open Doors project, 2022

HMP Feltham Park Run

With Geraint Thomas, Magnus Sheffield, Luke Rowe, 2023

First UTMB with the Alpine Run Project, 2023

With Andrew Graham and Chrissie Wellington at the Ministry of Justice

With AJ, Simon Cox, Terry Williamson and a PE teacher from Woodlands School

With Gavin from Sports Shoes and Charlotte Rawstron, Taylor Von Massey and Eleana Matos signing contracts with Sports Shoes

Dear John,

I write this letter to you after your visit in our prison in Oudenaarde.

I really appreciated your visit! I also had the feeling that I wanted to tell you more and talk to you more. But at the moment of your visit I was nervous and my English is not so fluent. So now I took my time to write down my thoughts in a letter.

First of all, I'm grateful you visited me. You kept your word and I really appreciated that. Most people look at us as 'the lowest of the society' and because of your visit I didn't feel like that anymore. You are also not just 'somebody', you are a triathlete and I really look up to you. And with your history as a prisoner, it has so much value to me.

Also, the fact you 'hugged' me several times gave me the feeling that you really listened and that you in one or another way wanted to be there for me, for us. And that motivated me really.

Everybody has highs and lows, you also were in prison and despite that you've made it this far. This gives me courage.

I also want to ask you to keep doing your job like you do now. Because you inspire people and the way you do it really makes sense for people like us. When I am outside the prison walls, and I have the possibility, I would really like to visit you. To do sport together and also because I want to let you know that your work really pays off. So you can see what your involvement did to me and how far I made it at that moment. For sure, you will hear from me when I'm free, if that's okay for you, and then I guess I will be less nervous ;-)

Thanks a lot for your visit! It meant a lot to me!

BIG D

Chapter 13

Virtual Reality

> 'Virtual Reality refers to computer-generated, three dimensional environments that stimulate real or imagined worlds, allowing users to interact with them as if they were present, often using special equipment like headsets and gloves with sensors to create an immersive experience.'
>
> **(Oxford Dictionary's definition)**

THE DRIVE from my place in Alpe d'Huez to the Nike HQ was 12 hours and everyone used to say to me, 'Why don't you just fly? It's so much quicker.' Let me explain. You can get a flight from Heathrow to Amsterdam in 45 minutes, but if I was leaving from my mum's, I'd drive from Kent to Dunkirk and then from there to the Nike HQ in Hilversum. The same went for this trip from Alpe d'Huez and numerous other trips. 'Why?' you ask. I personally thought it would be less problematic at that moment in time if I drove out instead of flying, because of the people I was around when I was in prison. I always thought that there's stuff still there in the background that could get me in trouble, and still do now, on occasions. Here's a few examples.

When I was in Belmarsh, during Ramadan, I was in this unit and you had the 21/7 suicide bombers and Abu Hamza. None of the prisoners were allowed to pray in the exercise yard during Ramadan, due to health and safety issues, and instead they had to pray in their cells. Then when they were finished, they were then allowed to go out into the exercise yard. On the main prison wing, there's hundreds of people, but where we were it was just a handful.

So, there we were in this big exercise yard, with only eight of us out there from the unit, which included myself and my mate, Roger Vincent. The 21/7 suicide bombers and Abu Hamza were praying in the corner and the prison officer was shouting, 'Get up. You're not allowed to pray there.' They ignored it and kept on praying towards Mecca. Me and Roger didn't give a shit about what was going on there and were just walking around, when suddenly the door to the exercise yard burst open. One of the prison officers had pressed the panic button and all the prison officers were now running across into the yard, with this lot praying behind us.

I said to the prison officers, 'They're not causing any fucking problems, just leave them.' We were now having an argument with the prison officers, and the governor came down as all these alarms were going off and they were still praying. I said, 'You're trying to bully them. Just let them pray. They're not causing anyone any harm and we're not going to trip over them. It's just us two walking around.' Then Roger started going mad as well.

By this point, they'd all stopped praying behind us and it was like a Mexican standoff with me, Roger and this lot behind us, and we were all arguing. The governor said, 'We don't want any problems. Go back to your cells. Exercise is finished.'

We walked back to our cells and were locked up. I thought that was the end of that, but next morning at 5am my door cracked open and they said, 'You're being moved.' I asked, 'Why?' They said, 'You're being shipped out.' They took me downstairs, strip-searched me, put me in that fucking boiler suit and then put me in the prison truck with an armed escort up to HMP Woodhill.

The problem was that nobody knew I was going there. I arrived about 8am and they had loads of people going to court and they didn't know where to put me, because I was double Cat A and couldn't go in a cell with most of the other prisoners. They had to put me in a cell with someone who was at my level of security. I was going mad saying, 'Why the fuck have I come here for?'

They chucked me into this cell and I sat down fuming, not paying attention to who was in the cell with me; then about two minutes later I heard all these running feet, the door cracked open and the guards said, 'McAvoy. Get out, now.' I thought, *They're gonna give me a hiding.* The guard shouted even louder, 'GET OUT, NOW!'

I got up and they slammed the cell door behind me. Because I was in such a raging zone, I didn't realise the person in the cell with me was Ian Huntley. He was going to court that morning for the murder of those two little girls in Soham.

They got me out of there, put me on a wing, and the Catholic priest asked what religion I was and all that. Then one of the principal officers came to my cell and I asked again, 'Why am I here?' He explained, 'You're being shipped out because you were about to start some sort of riot.' I said, 'Eh? What you talking about?' He said, 'You were in the exercise yard and you were one of the ringleaders.'

I put in a data protection request when I came out, and do you know what they put down in my security intelligence file? They said I was an Islamic supervisor and made out I was like a Jihadist. The moment I saw that I said, 'Get that out of my fucking file!' The problem was that I didn't get access to that file until I came out of prison, so that information followed me throughout my whole prison sentence. Not to mention, when I was in prison, Abu Hamza, even though he didn't have arms, he had pens on the end of these special hook things and he used to write me letters when I got moved to HMP Full Sutton. Just for the record, I never replied to any of them.

Another story. Babar Ahmad was being held under the Terrorism Act and was in prison the longest time without being sentenced. He was fighting extradition to the US, and when I went to Woodhill he came over and started talking to me. Long story short, he was released and he Tweeted me around 2020 and mentioned about how when he first met me in prison I was always a man of principles. He remembered when I stuck up for the Muslim brothers. I looked at that and once again thought, *Fuck that!*

Then there was a guy called Shaffi who tried to blow up the New York Stock Exchange, and he also tracked me down. He sent me a message and said, 'Oh my God, brother. Can't believe I found you and what have you been up to since getting out of prison?' Once again, *Fuck that!*

Then there was another guy, called Pablo, who had been in prison for nearly 40 years for drug importation. He contacted me and said he was in London and asked whether I would like to meet up with him. You've got it. *Fuck that!*

So, as you can understand, I've always been mindful of these kinds of things popping up and getting me in the shit at border control. So, the safer thing for me to do was to drive.

***

So, I was getting ready to drive up to Hilversum to pitch my idea for the Alpine Run, but ended up taking an intentional detour. Here's the background as to how and why that happened.

In early 2022 I approached a company called Zwift, who run a multiplayer online cycling programme that enables users to train, interact and compete with cyclists all over the world, but on a virtual platform. I went to them with an idea that was being linked into Feltham Young Offenders, where I was talking about technology in prisons and trying to get the youth prisoners involved by trying to race against people outside of prison. When I explained this to the Zwift team, they said, 'There's actually a project in Belgium that's been created at a prison outside of

Brussels, in a place called Oudenaarde. It connects prisoners to the outside world as anonymous athletes, giving them a sense of purpose and achievement, while helping them to reintegrate into the outside from prison.' And that's how I became aware of The Breakaway Project.

The initiative was being run in collaboration with the company Decathlon, and the guy heading up for them was called Fredrick, who was doing all Decathlon's PR and stuff. He asked, 'Would you be interested in doing an event with us?' He explained the project, and I said, 'One hundred per cent.' That's how it all came about, and it snowballed from there.

When the event took place in August 2022, there was about 100 people that took part. I was in Alpe d'Huez and there was my friend, Olympic gold medallist Mark Hunter, who was cycling from another location, and then there were people from all round the world. It was an amazing experience. Then after that ride, one participant, who we'll call Big D, wrote me a powerful letter saying how that ride impacted his life so much. He couldn't believe people cared about him and how sport had helped him turn around his outlook on life.

Then in October 2022 I now had a meeting scheduled to see Edgar at Nike HQ in Hilversum, but a couple of weeks before I felt this overwhelming need to see Big D and contacted the governor at the prison in Oudenaarde. I said, 'Would it be possible to meet one or more of the prisoners I did the ride with?' Thankfully, they said yes. At this point, Imogen Walsh was trying to see how Boats Not Bars could be delivered further afield and she also flew out for the visit, which gave her added perspective.

I went up to the prison to see this guy and, when I arrived, he was pleasantly shocked that he was seeing me in person and got emotional. He said, 'I can't believe you came. I also can't believe why so many people wanted to ride with me.' I wanted to meet him just to tell him we do care and that I want him to succeed in life and get his freedom back, which are emotions you don't get a great deal of when in prison. It was so powerful seeing him in person and being able to see the positive impact that event and sport has had on his life and mental health in prison. Afterwards, one of the prison officers sent me an email that said, 'I've never seen this man cry before. You really had an effect on him.'

After the event, I got in touch with Michele at HMP Feltham and explained what it was about, and eventually got them five Wattbikes donated, so they could do something similar, which was especially handy for them as they didn't have any money at the time in the prison.

Back to Oudenaarde. Me and Imogen stayed for a couple of hours and then I carried on driving up to Hilversum, while Imogen flew back to the UK. Next stop, the Netherlands.

Chapter 14

Selling the Dream

'Dare to live the life you have dreamed for yourself. Go forward and make your dreams come true.'

—Ralph Waldo Emerson

I LEFT Oudenaarde prison, jumped on the motorway and headed to Nike European HQ. When you arrive, you're surrounded by loads of inspirational slogans and buildings named after famous athletes such as Paula Radcliffe, and there's also a statue of Bill Bowerman, the guy who invented the first Nike shoe. I arrived, got my badge and Edgar came down and hugged me in the reception area. He then asked whether I wanted a coffee, so we went down to the canteen.

As we were about to walk up to his office, there was a lady called Samantha Rawlins, who was the head of running, and another guy called Tim Stuijfzand, who was head of Men's Marketing, and they were sitting having a meeting. Edgar took me over and said to them, 'Have you met John before?' They said, 'No.' I shook their hands and he then started talking about my life story.

Samantha looked at my feet and I had a pair of these old battered gold trail shoes on, which I called running slippers, because they were so comfortable. I became quite famous for this within Nike as I'm not materialistic and will wear a pair of trainers for thousands of kilometres. Sam asked, 'Do you like them?' I replied, 'Yeah. Love them. I've done two ultras in them and about a thousand kilometres in training. They're really comfortable.' You have to remember that they're used to working with people who change their shoes every four weeks. For me, it's a shoe that allows me to do what I love doing. The fact that I've done 2,000 kilometres in them is a good reflection of how durable they are.

Edgar said, 'I think you should come in on this meeting with John.' I went into the meeting with these three, and I said, 'Right, guys. I apologise for the quality of my PowerPoint presentation,' then started showing the slides. I almost ignored the visuals and just told the story. I said, 'I think there's an opportunity to change young people's lives by giving them the opportunities to take part in races like the UTMB kids' race. Trail running isn't like skiing, where you need a lot of money to engage in the sport, to buy skis, ski boots and ski passes. Trail running isn't a privileged sport. Where I live in the Alps, there's a lot of trail runners, many of whom are not rich at all, but have simply grown up in the mountains. They've been blessed with an amazing postcode.' As I was talking, I noticed Edgar smiling at me.

I left the room and thought, *Do they think I'm full of shit?* You have to understand that trail running was not a big part of Nike's running business at the time. Edgar then said, 'Do you know why I'm smiling?' and I said, 'No.' He explained, 'Last week we had an offsite meeting and every problem that we identified, you've given us a solution to. You've come in at the right time. In life, there's a right time and right place, and this is it for you. Let me go away and think about it, but would you come back here in another four weeks' time and speak at our running summit? There will be about 100 Nike Running team-mates from all over.' I agreed and Edgar said that would be a good time to announce the Alpine Run.

Four weeks later I went back with Jasper. We delivered the project more officially to Sam, Tim and the running team, and then afterwards I spoke at the running summit, where there were people from all over Europe and some people from Asia who were video-linked in.

Tim was interviewing me on stage and I pitched the idea to everyone. I said, 'We can do something different, but most importantly we can do something that can change these kids' lives authentically.'

I was asked several questions, such as, 'When did you start to run?' I replied, 'When I ran from London to Brighton. That was the first time I'd ever run. When I was in prison, I was surrounded by concrete and bars with very little human contact. I never saw a tree for ten years.' That got everyone's attention. I'm an athlete, not an employee, so I think it got them to challenge themselves to think differently of how they can change lives all around the world and inspire millions of people.

Sport builds resilience. It teaches you to lose, the benefits of how to adapt when you don't succeed in life and how you have to learn, move forward and not surrender to it. It also prepares you for how to deal with winning. If people engage with sport as kids, it can really set them up to achieve amazing things. For most of the kids coming on the project, the accomplishment of doing something so far out of their comfort zone is so empowering to them. We're not talking about getting kids on to the project who are elite-level athletes. For a lot of people who compete in sport to a high level, doing a marathon or riding 600km per week is no big deal but, to the majority, that could kill them if they did that every single week. Obviously, you build yourself up to that point, but when you take those challenges on as a young person and you think, *I can't do this. It's insurmountable*, but when you overcome it you realise how strong you actually are, pushing yourself outside of your comfort zone. You start to realise just how strong your body is, but more so how strong the mind is to be able to override the body when it wants you to stop. If you can take that mindset to other aspects of your life, you can be unstoppable.

There's a correlation between kids challenging themselves, eating healthily, being competitive and exercising, and how that translates to other areas of their lives when they get older. A lot of kids in state schools don't get that opportunity. They get something like 38 minutes of exercise per week. I've seen both sides of it. I've spoken at the most expensive private school in the UK, where it costs about 40 grand a year for each kid, and some parents have up to three or four of their kids there at the same time, which is about 150 grand a year in school bills. I'm sitting there with the kids and they're training in rowing or rugby for not far off 20 hours a week and they're not training dissimilar times to me. There's a reason why the school encourages it, because they realise how much it benefits them academically and how it teaches them those leadership skills to go on in their lives and be successful leaders.

With Alpine Run, we sent out an email to over 200 schools in Britain and only ten came back. I'm not digging out the schools or the teachers, because I understand the problem is that they're so stretched that they don't have the chance to respond to the Alpine Run Project in relation to their budget constraints. You do, however, then see a huge disparity between how one group of kids keeps growing and the others don't reach their true potential, because they don't get exposed to testing opportunities. That's why the Alpine Run is so important and that's why I was so passionate talking about it in Hilversum.

Thankfully, Nike bought in, backed it for the first year and put seed money in. From that moment I was already thinking, *That's great, but how are we going to build on this? I want to create something here that's not just a one-hit wonder.* That's when I brought JD Sports in.

JD was a strategic partner of Nike and at the time didn't do anything in running because they were seen as a lifestyle brand. We had to pitch it to Chris Edmends at JD before it was called Alpine Run, and at the time he worked for Nike, but was on the JD accounts as a senior director. I pitched the idea, they bought in and then became a joint partner with Nike in the first two years of Alpine Run, which in turn gave us that authenticity to the inner-city youth, because JD Sports had the direct channel into that group of people that we were trying to target. Once we had the people, we could then show them the mountains and trail running opportunities. That's how the project got off the ground.

We had 14 kids in that first year and at one point the Alpine Run was covered in every single newspaper in the UK. We even had a documentary on Amazon Prime in 2023 called *From the Streets to the Peaks*, and it won numerous awards, especially in North America, which consequently led to me receiving several messages from Americans about the project. For now, it was all about keeping the momentum of this initiative for future years.

Chapter 15

From Acorns Mighty Oaks Grow

'Someone once said, "Youth is wasted on the young." My response: "Not if I can help it."'

—John McAvoy

I WON'T lie, we went into the first Alpine Run Project in 2023 a little bit blind and let's just say it was a big learning curve for me and Jasper. After we had the green light from Nike, we decided to do a recruitment video, but we didn't have a media budget, so I kind of had to do a bit of gorilla marketing. In the video *From the Streets to the Peaks*, I said, 'I'm going to bring out ten young people to one of the most iconic trail running races in the world,' and see where it goes from there.

Jasper was amazing with Youth Beyond Borders running the social media page and leading on the recruitment and training programme, and I asked a lot of people I knew who had big presence on social media platforms to reshare and push it out on their channels. People like Tao Geoghegan Hart, who had won the Giro d'Italia; Jazz Carlin, the Olympic swimmer; boxer

Joshua Buatsi; and loads of others who were in the public eye. It also helped that I was able to get the national media on board, which really helped to push it and galvanise it. From there on, it became a snowball effect.

We received hundreds of applications that we didn't expect. Jasper said, 'Let's try and keep it to about 12 or 14 young people,' which made sense, but the problem was how to whittle down the applications. For the first Alpine Run we did all the interviews in person, which was ridiculously time-consuming but an invaluable experience. With that knowledge in hand, we were ready to take a more structured approach this time round.

We wanted a cross-section of society to make sure there were different backgrounds, gender, race, etc., but the most important thing was having people on board who we thought would really benefit from it. 'Why the Alpine Run Project?' and 'Why you?' If they said on their application form that they'd overcome any kind of significant barriers, that would get our attention. Some had grown up in care, being passed around the system; others had maybe suffered from health problems and some had maybe a bereavement to deal with. Whatever challenge they'd been handed in life, we wanted to see if the Alpine Run could help centre them moving forward in their lives.

After the interviews, we decided that we would tell the 14 successful candidates the good news on a live Zoom call. It was me, Jasper and a guy called Diego, who worked for Jasper. When everyone jumped on the call, they didn't know whether they'd been chosen or not and you could see the look of anticipation and nerves on their faces. We made a bit of a light-hearted note of it all and I built it up that they weren't coming.

Eleana Matos tells a funny story that she was really busy doing something at the time and had to stop to get on this Zoom call, then when I started talking and said, 'I'm sorry to say …' she thought, *What a waste of time. I should have carried on doing what I was doing, because he's just about to tell me that I'm not coming.* Then when I announced they were coming, everyone was relieved and ecstatic at the same time. People putting hands over their faces, a lot of smiles and a lot of screaming. Very memorable.

Now we had the candidates sorted we had to create and coordinate training camps, which ultimately worked towards the goal of the UTMB in Chamonix. In that first year, we organised hikes to places such as the Peak District, but we were learning off the cuff, and with time against us, we really had to shake, rattle and roll.

We wanted to give those who took part a sense of team identity, as we do now by giving them matching gear, which was kindly donated by Nike. However, there's also a balancing act with this, which comes down to my own moral compass. I really don't like materialism and I don't like incentivising materialism. The project fundamentally exists to take kids to nature. It isn't to give them free trainers, shorts and tracksuits. Even for my own kit allowance per year, I don't need thousands of pounds of gear. I get more satisfaction to gift that stuff to people who can't really afford it.

With the project, if we give them, say, a pair of £170 Nike trainers, they're not free, because someone is paying for that somewhere. I always say to the kids and the team, 'You have to treat the money that goes into the project like it's your own. You have to respect it when spending expenses.' We can't be frivolously spending money because it's there, and we're incentivising people and teaching them the wrong behaviours. We don't want kids applying purely on the fact that they see others decked out in all the flash gear. They need to earn that gear and not feel that because they've qualified on to the project that there's a sense of entitlement. 'Why am I not getting this?'

For many people, £170 is a lot of money and they can't afford to buy a pair of trainers every six months, but we don't want them to get into those habits of materialism. The gear gives them identity, and if they show they're helping each other and doing good in the community, instead of just wanting to meet the big names at the races, I make a mental note of that, because I know they're doing it for the right reasons.

We were very lucky that first year that we managed to create a really cohesive strong unit of people, which didn't cause us any problems, but it could have quite easily gone the other way. I think, because of the way we were with the young people and the way we cared about them and even when sometimes we felt they were deliberately doing things to make us drop them and push them away, which we never did, we built up their trust, which was a beautiful thing.

When we picked everyone, we wanted a 50/50 balance between boys and girls, a range of different backgrounds and, most importantly, that the Alpine Run Project could provide several firsts for everyone. Plus the blend of cultures and religions brought altogether in this group, which was amazing to watch. The best part is that most of them are still friends with each other now and many are ambassadors for the project.

With the candidates sorted, we also needed to let Sabina know, which came with its challenges. I know how frustrating it can be working with kids. You ask them to sign up to the UTMB … and they don't sign up. Then they give wrong email addresses, wrong dates of birth, etc., and UTMB is flat out doing all the PR for this massive global race and they've got a kid who isn't giving the information they need to register them into the race. They could easily have said, 'This is really difficult and we don't want to work with you,' but they didn't. The patience they showed us, and continue to show us, has been incredible. Also, despite a few complications about age, because for certain races you need to be 18 or over, for the youth aspect they managed to get those under 18 into the youth races that they run, to ensure each participant from our project would have the maximum sense of achievement running in the Alps.

For the first event, about four weeks after letting everyone know they were running in the UTMB, Sabina came to the Nike

HQ in London and met the kids to give a little talk to them about what to experience at the UTMB in the summer. Her team are amazing. That night, she was there with a girl called Jeann who worked for her, and Sabina was talking to the young people about what Chamonix was like, what to expect and how special this race was.

The race they were doing is called the UTMB YCC, which is two races in two days specifically for youth runners. The first race is in Italy and you go through the Mont Blanc tunnel, and then on the Wednesday they finish their second race in Chamonix, going through the big iconic finishing arch, with everyone clapping and cowbells being shaken by hundreds of supporters.

First day is 15km, with 1,200m of elevation. Wherever they're placed in that race, the following day is a time trial format. So, the slowest kid will start first and the fastest will go last, which in theory means that everyone would roughly be finishing around the same time, running through the arch in Chamonix.

It's a great way to get new trail runners to experience the magic of the mountains, and in this race they climb higher than the highest mountain in Great Britain, to the backdrop of the highest point in Europe. There's nowhere to hide and there's nothing that can really prepare you for it if you live in, say, London, Manchester or Birmingham. It's really difficult for the young people to fathom the scale and the gradient of the climb. Some really struggle and midway through will say, 'I can't do this,' while others are competing for podiums.

***

In preparation for the first UTMB, we did one training camp in the Peak District to introduce them to the sport and also gave them their first load of kit.

When taking a group of young people anywhere, there's health and safety considerations to be taken into account, but when you're heading into the mountains, in spaces where they take part in adventure, it's essential to have all bases covered. Jasper and Youth Beyond Borders were brilliant with managing risk and addressing any safeguarding challenges, in order to try to create a structure and process for young people to take part in.

With health and safety sorted, it was now time to get them into training, and let's just say there was a range of abilities. You got some people that are obsessed with the training and for others just moving and getting out was a massive achievement. Thankfully, I was able to get some help and support from a few athletes, such as Andrew Woodroffe.

I met Andrew by coincidence in a place called Thun, near Interlaken and Grindelwald, a beautiful part of Switzerland. I went riding over there with a friend of mine called Sophie Herzog, who was an ex-professional footballer for Switzerland and FC Zürich, and she mentioned about this coach who had moved to Zürich: 'Would you mind if he came and joined us for this ride?' I replied, 'No problem.'

That's when I first met Andrew. He was a triathlon coach for Triathlon Scotland at elite level and then he got a job in Zürich with their development squad for the under-23 triathletes. We built up a rapport that day, stayed in contact with each other, then he came out to Alpe d'Huez to do a triathlon race with his mate and we did a few rides together. Then when I was putting the Alpine Run Project together, we wanted to bring in a coach, because I didn't want to go down that route of coaching the kids as well, because that would have been too much for me to take on. I asked Andrew and he said, 'It would be an absolute honour.'

Andrew started coaching the group, but what I noticed quite quickly was that, if you're someone like Eleana and you have the opportunity with the sport element, they want to see how quick they can run as athletes in the UTMB. So, bringing someone of Andrew's stature into the camp was like a big lightbulb moment, because people like Eleana understand the value of what that person has done. However, that wasn't the case with some of the other kids. If you said, for example, that you won an Olympic gold in rowing, they wouldn't care, because they couldn't relate to that whatsoever. As a result, that became quite frustrating for Andrew after writing a training programme out, which some of the kids wouldn't follow. He's used to working with type-A personalities where you've got to hold them back from themselves. You don't want them to do more, you're trying to get them to do less, because they're so driven. It was a learning curve for me and interesting to observe.

We realised as the project progressed that you've got to find ways to coach these kids from where they're starting from and that's why we've now started working with an organisation called New Levels Coaching, with Lewis Moses and Gemma Hillier-Moses. They can coach up to an elite level, which they do, but they've got a good skills base to be able to work with weekend warriors. This in turn allows the kids who are just starting off on their running journeys to feel less stressed and pressured.

Back to the first Alpine Run recruits. I think the key to working with so many different levels of ability is all about trying to validate the needs of the young people and making sure they get something out of it because they feel affirmed and valued. Does it work? Mostly, yes. There's some, though, that turn up to the most challenging environments in Europe, if not the world, without doing enough training and we've almost had to carry them over the finish line, but longer term they've got a sense of achievement and accomplishment that they've done something during that six months that before they would never have believed was possible.

One thing we insisted on was that everyone had to eat together and cook together. Everyone got a training plan and within that there was nutritional advice, so by the time they got to Chamonix, they were tuned to healthy eating. If they were really keen, like Eleana, then we would signpost them to performance coaches. One of the big challenges has been that some of the runners get a runner's high and they get addicted to it. The problem is that they're young and still growing, so a big thing has been about managing their training programmes and expectations so they don't run too much. They get so much into a buzz that it can get excessive, so it's essential to manage that.

Toby Hunter's wife, Kirsty, acted as a massive support for the first Alpine Run Project. She's a really compassionate, lovely woman, a trained professional in mental health and wellbeing care for youngsters, and the kids from that first year still talk about her. I've always said to Toby, 'You're a very, very lucky man!' You have to remember that the first year we deliberately picked a group of kids who had numerous issues in their lives, and I'm not an expert on that side of things. Trying to use logic doesn't always work, because some of the kids' thinking was irrational, but Kirsty, with her background of working for many years with kids in schools, proved to be very useful in terms of what's needed to provide due care for kids.

For example, there was a girl on the project who had come through Gloves Not Gunz and we'd brought her on and realised quite quickly that she wasn't ready yet. We made the decision before the first year race that she would be excluded, because it would be safer that way, due to her fitness. However, we still let her come and she ended up being the cook for the group that week, with Kirsty mentoring her and others throughout the week. Although she didn't run, it was amazing to see her grow and develop in another way. On a similar parallel, it was also an interesting journey for me on development and growth.

One thing I could certainly bring to the table was experience, on several levels. The race, the environment and being prepared for success and failures. The first time I pulled out of a race was when I pulled out of the UTMB Nice due to a viral infection. I got to 85km of a 111km race and I started feeling like I was going to faint, so pulled out at a checkpoint. At the time you think it's the end of the world, but years later I realised it was just my ego being challenged. I'd got that far, was doing really well, in the top 20, but then started to get the little white dots appearing and pulled out before I passed out. I take it as a reflective experience and learn from it. Year two, I made a lot of changes to reduce the probabilities of these things happening again. If I can pass this knowledge to the young people, it will help them face dissatisfaction and disappointment positively.

Some kids were worried about altitude, but I reassured them by explaining that it only starts to occur from about 3,000 metres and above, and because Chamonix sits around 1,000 metres above sea level, we were in a relatively comfortable zone. However, one thing that they all agreed on when coming out to the Alps was the purity of the air. Many of them had never experienced anything like it before, having only ever lived in places like London, with all the pollutants floating around. Same goes for light pollution. The kids were going out at night and they couldn't believe how many stars they could see, which again you'd never see in London.

As far as the race itself goes, I wanted them to be excited for what they were taking part in, but to keep a level head. The UTMB can be like Disneyland on steroids and a real contrast to me wanting to connect them to the tranquillity, peace and serenity of the mountains. Chamonix gets caught up in this massive slipstream for the days the UTMB is on, and most of the people on the streets are either wearing hiking or trail running gear, and every single person encourages a runner as they go past. The sound of the cowbells through the night and day are being rung by the old and the young, with colour, race and creed never being distinguished for every runner that is heading towards the finishing line. When my guys started and finished the race, the most important thing for me was that they felt present with the experience after all the hard work they'd put in, getting them to the finish line.

***

Lessons learned from the first Alpine Run? There was definitely a lot of things that needed fine-tuning. When you look back, I wanted to take 14 young people, who had never run, to the mountains to do one of the biggest trail races in the world, which is amazing, but it doesn't really work to take a handful of people who have never run. We had six months to train but they'd never run, so they didn't know how to train correctly.

In the beginning it was a bit up in the air, but now we've structured an itinerary that always starts with young people going out to green spaces, but close to where they live. So, if they're in London, that might be the Surrey Hills, and if they're in Manchester, that could be the Lake District; then one or two national summits, usually in the Peak District, where they all come together. Those were organised in the early days, quite close to the times, on a month-by-month basis, but now we've got an annual programme of events that always culminates with the mecca of running, which is Chamonix and going to the UTMB at the end of August each year.

When the project wrapped up in year one, I was mindful that I didn't want to give preferential treatment to any of the participants, so I tried to nurture each one of these kid's interests that I was able to help with. For example, with Marek I helped to introduce him to Nike marketing, and with Eleana I was trying to help open doors for the progression of her running, more so as an athlete, not just a participant of the project.

I spoke with Eleana and said, 'What you need is financial renumeration, which will help you and your mum go to races. You need to be in some campaigns, because that will elevate you as an athlete.' She said, 'I'll follow your lead.'

I went back to Nike, explained what I wanted for Eleana and they agreed to give her some financial renumeration and some kit allowance. I then asked her, 'What can I do to help you progress? What is it you think you lack?' She replied, 'Things like training camps and being around elite athletes.' I said, 'Let's do some training camps next year.'

The disadvantage these kids have, not living where I do, is massive. The kids from up in the mountains are living 365-day training camps and are picked up by massive trail brand sponsors as teenagers. With Eleana, it was about 'how can we close this gap?' You can't expect her to learn her craft running the streets of, say, Manchester and then run in Chamonix. She needs to be in the mountains training. Taking her out to these environments and giving her exposure will improve her running.

Eleana picked two girls from the project to come with her, then we organised the camp in Girona and she came out to the Alps in the summer of 2024, where we did high-altitude training. It's given her more exposure to exactly what she wanted: training camps and being around some of the most elite-level athletes on the planet. However, the rest of the year didn't run so smoothly for me.

Chapter 16

Hip-Hop

'They're funny things, accidents. You never have them till you're having them.'

—A.A. Milne

I WAS down the south of France for a couple of months, training for the 2024 Istria 100, which is organised by UTMB. I was training alongside the likes of Geraint Thomas, Luke Rowe, a pro rider of 20 years, Magnus Sheffield, an American kid who rides for Ineos, and Tom Watson, who's also part of Ineos. I was really looking forward to the training as I'd planned this trip ages ago, and being around these guys would give me such a boost to my training.

With the event only a few weeks away, my mate Terry came over, and by this stage I was absolutely flying alongside this lot with high-intensity training. I went to pick him up from Nice airport and we drove back to the place I was staying in Villefranche-sur-Mer, which is where the Rolling Stones used to have a big recording studio. Thirty minutes later, we were at the digs, but I wasn't feeling it and just needed a little break from training. I had calls to make, and Terry's very independent, so I said to him, 'Tel, go out and ride and we'll catch up later.' He said, 'Don't worry. I'll wait for you.' I didn't want to be rude, so after I made these calls, I got my cycling kit on and we started the ride.

We left the Airbnb and only five minutes later I'm in front, Terry's behind me, I'm riding down the road and the traffic lights in front of me went red. The car in front of me chucked the brakes on, so I put on my brakes, and just as I'm about to unclip my foot from the pedal, Terry smashed right into me. He missed my back wheel, tried to go round me at the last second, but hit my inside pedal, where my foot was still locked in. I wasn't expecting it, so I crashed to the floor, but wasn't able to put my arms out to brace the fall.

I got up and straight away the pain was really bad. I've got a high pain threshold, but I'd never experienced anything like this. I had to sit down on a wall and could hardly put any weight at all on that leg. I was semi-fuming because I was supposed to be racing three weeks later in Croatia. Terry felt really bad. I said, 'Mate. It was an accident. Let's just get going.' I got back on the bike and we were riding, but I could feel something was really not right around my hip. As you ride into Nice, there's this long climb called Col d'Èze, and as we started going up that, I couldn't put any pressure on the leg and Terry pulled away from me and rode off.

Shortly after, Terry turned around, came back down and asked, 'Sure you're alright?' I said, 'Something's wrong with my leg. This doesn't feel right. You go and ride. Leave me alone and I'll meet you back where we're staying.' That's always been what I do in life. I just need some time to be left alone, retract, analyse and then make a decision. I need that time of solitude to reset and work out how I can overcome the situation.

I started cycling back and by now the adrenaline had gone and the pain ramped right up. The area I was staying in was all really old buildings and I had about 200 steps to walk up to my accommodation. When I got off the bike, I couldn't put an ounce of weight on my left leg and had to crawl, one step at a time, dragging my bike up with me. It took me about 20 minutes to get up 20 flights of stairs. I put my key in the door, went into the living room and took my cycling shorts off. The whole of my left side was badly bruised.

My good mate Aidan O'Flaherty is a physio, so I contacted him and explained what had happened and what was wrong. He started laughing and said, 'Hang up the call and let's do a videocall.' I called him back and he was trying to do an assessment of me and said, 'Stand up.' I stood up, but put all my weight on my right leg. He then said, 'Now I want you to hop.' Although I was able to hop on my right leg, the pain on my left-hand side was excruciating. He then said, 'You need to have an X-ray. I don't think you've broken it, because you're not in pain when you're sitting down, but I think you might have fractured it.'

I got in the shower, turned the water on and all the cuts and grazes on my arms and legs started stinging as the water made contact. It took me ages to get out of the shower because I couldn't use any bodyweight to swivel, so I held on to the shower wall and finally managed to get over to the sofa. By this stage, Terry had come back, and I said, 'Mate, I think I need to go to hospital. I might have fractured something. But listen – let me go to bed tonight and see how I feel tomorrow morning, and if I still feel like now, then I'll go.'

I had the worst night's sleep, as the hip was pulsating, and the next morning I said to Terry, 'I'm fucked. I need to have this X-ray.' I didn't want him to come with me as I just wanted to deal with it myself, as it was my problem, but Terry kindly insisted and drove me to the hospital in Nice. My hip was X-rayed and the nurse said, 'It's not broken.' I replied, 'There's nothing else you can see?' She said, 'No.' Terry was so relieved.

While I was walking with a track pump as a crutch, I could hardly cross the road, because as I was walking I'd get stuck with a shooting pain. We went back to the Airbnb, and the day after Terry headed back to the UK. I had to go to Girona in Spain to do a photoshoot with Nike in four days' time, which I couldn't do. One of the kids from Alpine Run was coming out for it, so I said to Nike, 'I'll do my best to come, but never mind running for this shoot, I can't stand on my leg.'

Four days later, I was able to hobble, but it was taking me about ten minutes to do 20 metres, which was really pissing me off. I drove from Nice to Girona, which wasn't the easiest or cleverest idea, and when I got out of the car in Girona I had to walk from my car to the Airbnb. I was constantly stopping, and my jaws started aching because I was biting down so hard in pain.

Aidan said to me from London, 'If the X-ray shows no break, you should get an MRI, which might identify a fracture.' I booked this MRI in Girona, explained to the nurse what had happened, and about 40 minutes later I was told, 'You've fractured your hip socket.' She then asked, 'How long have you been walking around like that?' I said, 'A week and a half.' She shook her head and said, 'What pain relief medication have you been taking?' I replied, 'None.' She said, 'That's remarkable. You should have been in an air cast. Go and see a physio as soon as you can.'

I went to see a physio who works with all the top cyclists and she was also bemused with how I'd managed to walk with this fracture. She also said that my powers of recovery were brilliant, because most people wouldn't be able to walk for a month. Within six weeks, I was running again and made a full recovery.

That was the first bone I'd ever broken or fractured in my life. Years ago, Nike sent me to a research lab in Belgium, just outside Antwerp, and I had the whole lot done. Cardio scanner, bone density, you name it. The guy that was doing it asked me about my training history and I explained that I covered X number of kilometres a year on my bike and running, with this amount of elevation, I've done millions of metres on an indoor rowing machine, I walk and I used to swim 20km a week. When he looked at my scans he said that my tendons and ligaments were absolutely fine, which was strange, bearing in mind what I put my body through. He believed that taking up sport when I was 26 was a big factor, because my body was fully developed and that means my body age is much more robust than some who start sport early. I have to laugh, though, because up to the point where Terry wiped me out, I'd dodged bullets on more than one occasion, but never so much as pulled a muscle. I still laugh with Terry about this now. He might be my informal agent and a best mate, but he did fracture my hip!

***

Thankfully, 2024 had some less painful memories that I'll cherish for life.

Cam Wurf rowed for Australia at the 2004 Olympics in Greece, then became a professional road cyclist, before becoming an Ironman competitor. Cam had watched the Red Bull documentary I'd done in 2018 and then we started a dialogue online. He was on a camp in Sierra Nevada, Spain with Geraint Thomas, had read my book during that camp and then passed it to Geraint. Geraint read the book, got my number from Cam and one day I received a random WhatsApp saying, 'Hope you don't mind me messaging, it's Geraint Thomas. Would you be interested coming on my podcast?' I replied, 'Yeah. Definitely.' Geraint is famous for winning the Alpe d'Huez Stage in the Tour de France in the yellow jersey and then winning the whole Tour de France later, which was the first time that was ever done. Also, the Tour de France only comes through Alpe d'Huez about every four or five years.

So, I did the podcast in 2022 with him and we were messaging sporadically. Then in 2023 the Tour de France was back in Alpe d'Huez and he messaged me about a week before to ask whether I had any suggestions for accommodation for his wife and their little kid, because they were struggling to find anywhere. I linked him up with some friends who had an apartment and they stayed there. When the Tour was done, he was having some downtime and he messaged me again: 'Me and my family and my family-in-law are looking to come to Alpe d'Huez. Anyone you know who could accommodate that number? My wife has booked something up, but wondered if you might have any suggestions?' I replied, 'Yeah. I know a couple of people. Let me ask them.' I ended up finding them somewhere cheaper through a friend and they got a big chalet.

When they got out here, he said, 'Do you want to do a couple of rides?' I replied, 'One hundred per cent, mate.' He came out and we did a bit of riding with his father-in-law and then we agreed to do a ride on the Saturday. However, that didn't go as smoothly as either of us had planned.

On the Friday night I went out to a Thai restaurant down at the bottom of the valley where I live and I had the worst food poisoning I've ever had in my life. I woke up in the middle of the night vomiting and was so, so sick. I was supposed to be riding with Geraint at 10am and, if it had been anyone else, I would have bowed out, but because it was him I got ready. Honestly, though, I looked like Casper. Powder-white with black rings under my eyes.

Geraint came over to mine and he needed help with his bike, because his back wheel had blown up and he needed a mechanic to put the tyre on, as it was a special tubeless one. Ollie at the bike shop said, 'Bring it in,' and all he wanted in return was a picture with Geraint after fixing it. The funny thing was that Geraint had a raging hangover from the night before, after going out with his family, and was also feeling a bit fragile, but neither of us said anything for this three-and-a-half-hour ride. It was probably one of the worst rides I've ever done. I was pushing power numbers that were hardly anything, but my heart rate was going through the roof, not to mention every time I was drinking water I was spewing up all over my bike, but thankfully he didn't see that because I was cycling behind him. Geraint, in the meantime, was battling this epic headache. Neither of us wanted to ride, but neither of us wanted to let the other person down.

As we were riding, he started to feel better, cycling off the hangover, while I was feeling worse. As we were riding up the Col de Sarenne, up the back of Alpe d'Huez, we started talking a little bit more, and after the ride I explained that I felt like shit: 'If it wasn't riding with you, I would have never done this,' and he smiled and said, 'I didn't want to come out either!' He then explained about the session he'd had the night before. We both erupted into laughter.

We stayed in contact, and in 2024 he was down in Monaco while I was staying in Villefranche-sur-Mer, in the south of France, for about six weeks. It's an absolutely beautiful setting, right on the ocean between Monaco and Nice, in this little harbour. As you come out, you get straight back into the mountains and into a climb. All of the top pro cyclists in the world live around that area, and when you go out riding, you'll never see so many elite cyclists in one place. I went down there and let Geraint know I was in the neighbourhood, and he said, 'Great. Do you want to tag along with us?' I said, 'Yes!'

We were riding up the Col de la Madone (translates as Pass of the Madonna), which is a really famous cycle route, due to how challenging a climb it is. You come out of the south of France and head down to a place called Menton. All the pro riders use that mountain to test their fitness. I had a pinch-myself moment as I was riding with Geraint, Luke Rowe and Magnus Sheffield. We were starting to descend as a group and were doing about 60kph on the flats, sweeping round these roads. It was a euphoric moment, but it was more a moment of reflection, realising once again how far I'd come from being in prison and watching the Tour de France from behind bars, to suddenly riding with someone who had won the Tour, and all these other top pro riders, up this iconic mountain ride. This all came about because of decisions and choices I made in my life and continue to make. Life is all about being true to yourself, because you can lie to as many people as you want, but the man in the mirror will always know if you've made a right decision.

Chapter 17
I Ain't No Car Salesman

> 'I don't wear Adidas, I'm a Nike guy. I'm a Nike guy. So I'm so excited about being a Nike guy, I just felt that was the best fit for me.'
>
> **—LeBron James**

WHEN I was in prison, the general public and the system didn't want to be anywhere near me, which I understand, simply because of the person I was back then. However, I now get asked on a weekly basis to either endorse a product, make an appearance somewhere or basically do something that goes against my ethics in what I believe in life. That's of no interest to me whatsoever.

My wealth nowadays is my success and that's certainly not about being rich financially. I've been asked to go on *Big Brother*, and when I tell people I've turned it down, they probably think I make fortunes to be able to do that, but I really don't. My outgoings are not that great, because I don't live an ostentatious lifestyle. I live in a basic flat in Alpe d'Huez and my needs are very few. When people come to see me, they ask, 'Have you just moved in?' I say, 'No. I've been here for a few years.' They then say, 'But you've hardly got anything in here.'

The world of business can be very cutthroat and I'm not willing to trample over or backstab people who have helped me turn my life around, just for the sake of money. I've never wanted to work with an agent and have always done everything off my own back. I make my decisions based on what I feel in my heart and always said when I got released from prison that I would never make a decision based on money.

Although Terry Williamson hates to be called my agent, at times he's done exactly what an agent does, except he doesn't take a single penny for all his hard work. He's the opposite of how a traditional agent operates as so many of them appear to think, *What money can I get from this deal? Then I'll take my cut and it's happy days.* We make decisions based on far more important subject matters, and he gets that. He helps to guide me with decisions that could have potentially crucified my position and outlook. I think that if I had someone else instead of Terry, they may have said, 'Oh, maybe do just this one, John,' then I would lose all self-respect and credibility of everyone I work with. When an offer is of interest to me, Terry negotiates the money to make sure I get the maximum benefit from it, but he'd never push me into anything.

Here's a few examples. Let's start with the approach from the loan company. Terry got this email asking if I would endorse a certain product. He phoned me up and was laughing when he said, 'John, this opportunity has come in.' I said, 'What is it?' He said, 'A burglar alarm company.' We both started laughing.

The brief was a day's shoot, where they wanted me to do the advert, and then half a day of doing interviews with the press and another half a day prerecording radio interviews. I said straight away, 'No.' Terry said, 'Do you want me to tell you how much it is?' I said, 'Go for it, but it won't change anything.' The offer was for 25 grand, for roughly two days' work, but I refused it.

Someone said to me before, 'You sell ideas, not products,' and that's totally true. I don't sell trainers for Nike or bikes for Cervelo. I don't want to sell overly materialistic things and certainly didn't want to sell burglar alarms and become a caricature of myself. The way I am with my life, it can make things difficult for me, because I can be at a financial loss. Twenty-five grand was and still is a lot of money, especially as that was more than I was earning in a year at the time and was the largest amount of money I would have received since being out of prison.

Here's another example I turned down, but this one was massive. One day, a friend of mine, who knew such and such, had mentioned that this guy was interested in putting a sponsorship deal together for me. We knew the agency, who the person was and the fact that his aim would be to earn as much money as possible irrespective of the wellbeing of my aims in life. Out of interest, we decided to go to see him.

We got to these plush offices and sat down. The guy who had introduced us was in the room, but silent. I introduced Terry as someone who was there just as a support, because he hated being called an agent, but also Terry's skills at these meetings are not to say much but watch the others and interpret. The guy putting the deal together said, 'The fastest way to make someone marketable is to put them on telly, because then you are in people's homes. I can see an opportunity to create a programme, with the likes of BBC2, going round to people, using sport to stop kids from committing crime and that can then lead to other opportunities for you to go on other TV programmes. You'll then become a household name and you can make money out of public speaking.' This was all well and good, but it would obviously benefit him financially as well.

This agency had worked with some massive athletes, and he asked, 'Can you tell me what Nike are paying you?' I replied, 'No, I'm not doing that.' He asked, 'Why not?' I said, 'Well, firstly, it's confidential, and secondly, this is an initial meeting and I don't feel comfortable telling you.'

I was working with the greatest sporting brand the world has ever seen, who had worked with some of the best athletes that ever walked the Earth, but more than anything, they took a chance on me when many were turning away. That meant more to me than money. He said, 'I think you've got a rose-tinted outlook on what Nike is. Do you want me to tell you what I think you're worth?' Terry looked at me and then looked at this guy and said, 'Yeah. What do you think he's worth?' This guy said, 'I think you are worth a hundred grand a year and I can get you a three-year contract with another brand.' I said, 'No, I don't want it.' He asked, 'Why not?' I replied in a very respectful manner, 'But what can they do for me?' I'd talked about all of this stuff of helping people and supporting kids and wanted to know how they would help with that. The guy didn't get it at all and just wanted my name and face for the brand. He'd probably never even been challenged before and was a bit taken back by me not biting his arm off for the money.

There were only a few months of that Nike contract left at the time, but I know now, if I would have taken that deal, I would not be in the position I am today. Also, the relationships I formed with people like Toby, Dan, Edgar – those relationships allowed me to do so much good with my life and they believed in me so much and stuck their necks out for me. The old John McAvoy would have taken the money. 'Three hundred grand over three years? Yeah. Fuck it, I'll take that.' It comes back to me being a kid and having that sense of loyalty. If you're good to me, I'll be good to you. That's never left me and I won't stab people in the back because someone's come along and dangled a big financial offer in front of me.

However, not all approaches are bad. Without Nike, my life would be different and what I've been able to achieve for the young people would have been much harder and no way near the scale I've been able to deliver on so far. Same goes with numerous other sponsors such as Cervelo and Volvo. Let me tell you a nice story about Volvo.

In 2019, Terry received an email to my website and it was from an agency called CAA (Creative Artists Agency), who are one of the biggest agencies on the planet. They said, 'We are working on behalf of a car brand and we were wondering if you have any contractual obligations with any other car manufacturers?'

Terry went back to them and explained that I wasn't working with anyone at the time, but also asked the car brand in question. They said, 'We can't tell you at the moment. We just wanted to see whether John had any connections to other car brands.'

There was a bit of back and forth on emails and then they asked me to sign a non-disclosure agreement, so they could tell me the brand. Shortly after, they told me it was Volvo. I thought, *Wow*, but I did also think, *I made it clear from the very beginning that I was happy to have a chat with them, but I hope they realised I wasn't a car salesman, as in I didn't intend to start selling the brand.* I didn't want to start driving around doing videos saying, 'Wow, this is the best car in the world, it handles great, has lovely seats and everyone needs to buy it.' I don't sell stuff. That's not what I do. They replied, 'No, no. That's not what we want to do. We want it to be an organic, authentic relationship between the two of us. We're doing some stuff with triathlon and thought this could be a nice fit for both of us.'

I really enjoyed working with Volvo, because they were true to their word. Here's a few examples. I got invited to the Kendal Mountain Film Festival in 2019 and did a short film with them, which was about announcing my partnership with them.

It was a one-and-half-day shoot in the Surrey Hills, with me riding my bike and driving the Volvo, but it was more about the story of me and Darren, and how sport had changed my life, as opposed to me talking about the leather interior or how quickly it accelerated.

Once the film had been made and was all set to be launched at the Kendal Mountain Film Festival, I asked them whether I could take some kids from FBB. They agreed and Jasper came up with them on a Friday evening. That night, the day before the film launch, we all went out for dinner and there was me, Jasper, two of the young people from FBB, Miguel and Deborah, and a lady called Jenny Smith who headed up marketing at Volvo, plus all the CAA team.

The kids were sitting either side of me, and that night reiterated the importance of giving these kids access to these worlds that they might not normally get access to. When we started looking at the menu, Miguel said to me, 'What can I have?' I said, 'You can have anything you want.' He pointed to the menu and said, 'But that steak costs £40.' You have to remember that Miguel lives in a council flat in south London, so that was a lot of money for him to get his head around, especially for a plate of food. I replied, 'If that's what you want, mate, then order it. You can have it.' His eyes went wide open and he checked with me a few times to make sure I wasn't joking.

My friend Rebecca Scown, who was double Olympic medallist, also came up and was with the kids, asking them questions about FBB and their interests in life. I have to say, the kids were amazing and were interacting with everyone at the table. We had a great dinner and then we all went back to our hotel rooms, went to bed. Then the next morning we went to do a well-known trail run before the film was played in the afternoon in front of about 150 people. I was there with a para athlete called Lauren Steadman, who Volvo were sponsoring, and we were on stage doing a Q&A, while the kids were sat at the front of the audience with Jasper. The kids were given the VIP treatment by Volvo and were mesmerised by the whole experience. From that event, my relationship with Volvo flourished, even during testing times.

When Covid happened, I was still living in Putney and Volvo had given me the use of an SUV, which was worth about 50 or 60 grand, but it was sitting outside doing nothing. At the time, I was doing some work with a children's hospice and the lady I knew from the hospice said they were really struggling to take these bottles of oxygen to those in need, because they didn't have enough cars. I got in touch with Volvo and said, 'I don't need this car at the moment. It's just sitting there doing nothing. Can I gift the car and let them use it?' They replied straight away, 'Yes. No problem.' It was little things like that which really meant a lot to me, and when Alpine Run was getting off the ground they were going to give me a fleet of Volvos to take the kids up to the mountains. All this stuff was lined up and then Covid blocked it.

Volvo were so nice to work with. I went to speak at their UK distribution centre in front of all their senior leadership team, and I really liked the partnership I had with them and the relationship I'd built up with them. I was genuinely sad when the relationship ended in 2022, and I mean that, but I understand that it's business, and marketing budgets get moved elsewhere and cutbacks have to be made, and I was just one of those people.

Then when the Covid lockdown finished in 2023, a guy called Frazer Riley from Strava reached out, wanting to work with me as an athlete. I had a call with him and he said, 'You live in Alpe d'Huez, which is a spectacular place, and your Strava activity is incredible.' I was training every single day and was a great example of someone who used their app every day to monitor their training, for years.

Initially, I wasn't interested, just because I wanted fewer obligations in my life, not more, but I then started to think about the kids on the Alpine Run and the fact that most of them don't know what Strava is when they join the project. In fact, we have to do workshops to explain what the app does and how to install it on their phones. Looking at the wider picture, I said to Frazer, 'I've set up this project called the Alpine Run and we did our first year this year.' I started telling him some stories, and you could tell he was genuinely touched by them. I asked if he could help amplify the project and get the message out, maybe get Strava to help share the application form next year to the kids, because they have millions of followers.

He went away to his team and he brought in this lady called Amy Stanton-Foo, who was based in Chamonix and spread her working time between the UK and France. She's an amazing woman and was fantastic at the marketing aspect of things. When you help amplify what's going on with the Alpine Run, that in turn helps more brands to get involved, which means more capital, which means more opportunity. One of my sales pitches now is that Alpine Run has been in every single major national newspaper and magazine in the UK, other than the tabloid press. From a business perspective, that makes the project very appetising for any potential investors.

Strava funded our project in Chamonix in 2024 when we did the Next One Wins event at La Folie Douce hotel, part-funded by them and Nike. I was on stage with them, but the event was very youth-led by all the kids on the Alpine Run Project, talking about their experience of having the opportunity to engage in trail running. They've been really good for us and are more of an amplification partner than a financial investing partner, but for us it's very beneficial from an added value perspective.

The day after, I was chatting to one of the guys who set up The Great Run series and he said that when one of the guys from the project got up on stage and took to the microphone, he thought he was a young Nike employee introducing the project. Then when he saw a photo of him running, he was blown away. It just goes to show what can happen when you give kids a platform, but more importantly the confidence to speak on that platform.

With the skills and the knowledge, these kids can be amazing. It's all about opportunities. That's really important to me. However, opportunities often come with doors being opened for you, and I'll never forget those who helped me on my journey.

Chapter 18

You Still in Touch with That Geezer? The One from the Nick?

'Your friends will know you better in the first minute you meet than your acquaintances will know you in a thousand years.'

—Richard Bach

BY 2017, I'd got into a routine with Marilyn, my probation officer, that I was allowed to leave the UK on short breaks to do training camps, because she understood the value they would add to me as an athlete. Despite doing a lot of endurance racing in cycling and running, Darren Davis had never done an Ironman before 2014; that's until I convinced him. Then in 2015 he did his first full Ironman in Bolton and then a couple of Half Ironmans in 2016, followed by the full Ironman in Weymouth in 2016.

Back to 2017. At the time, there was a camp going on at Lake Annecy, which somebody else was organising, and I asked, 'Can I bring my friend, Darren?' This guy said, 'Yeah. Not a problem.' Terry was also on it, along with a few other mates. People asked me whether bringing Darren out felt strange, but for me it was a great story in so much as I was going away to a foreign country with a prison officer that used to lock me up!

Darren loved it. We ran together, swam, cycled and he also did his own bits, while I was focused on getting ready for the Ironman race, which was six weeks after the camp. Since then, I've lost count the number of times we've been away with each other. Peak District, Lake District, France about four or five times, Germany, you name it.

Then, in 2021, Darren left the prison service after just over 21 years working in the system, and the fact that we now work with each other mentoring young people is a beautiful thing. Darren helped me to learn about the power of giving back and helping other people. He demonstrated to me in prison that you need someone to believe in you, help you, give you the tools to unlock your own talents and do something with them. Without him, I wouldn't be the man I am today, and it's not just about what I've done physically, it's the things he's taught me and the friendship we've created.

When the Alpine Run Project started to come together, Darren slowly but surely became a big support to me and the young people involved. In 2024 I asked him to take them on a hike in the beautiful countryside of the Peak District, and without hesitating he agreed. He went out there, did a reccy of a stunning 14km hike that finished along the river, which for many of the kids would have been their first experience outside of their postcode, walking along trails with steep inclines and jumping into streams. Darren successfully took them out of their comfort zone and got them to understand themselves and the team they were a part of. I wasn't there, but what I've noticed over the years is that the kids love it, because they know about Darren and his relationship with me, so when they get to meet him, it's a big thing for them.

Then in April 2025, me and Darren presented evidence to the Times Crime and Justice Summit. There were loads of really bigwigs there, including the head of the prison service, head of probation service, the crime correspondent from *The Times* newspaper and two High Court judges. Basically, the movers and shakers in the criminal justice system in the UK, and *The Times* commissioned this report to change the criminal justice system. I had police officers, prison officers, judges in a room in London all asking me questions about my journey, which again was strange as I'd never have imagined the people who wanted to lock me up were now asking for my advice.

One of the things that Darren said was for officers to go back into the community, to be that familiar face, that mentor and trusted person and to see how they're doing. That's what he did with me, and he's always said to me, 'I'm always there for you. I'll support you.' I also talked a lot about mentorship, but not as an athlete, but how, precisely, Darren helped me to change my life. The mindset of prison officers when joining the prison service should be: 'We're going into this job to change people's lives, not lock them up.' That was Darren's mentality, and if others did the same, the criminal justice system could change quite substantially. Also, retaining people like Darren is essential, which means you need to treat them well and pay them well, but sadly that side of things lacks massively.

The truth is that without Darren opening the door of opportunity for me, making me realise I had potential, I wouldn't have set those records on a rowing machine and my life wouldn't have panned out the way it did. As a result, my life story wouldn't have been shared and other prisoners wouldn't have had a relatable blueprint of how to change their lives positively through sport behind bars. Here's a lovely recent example.

A prisoner on Mike Crofts's 3Pillars programme, Ben Ellett, went into prison weighing nearly 120kg, while standing at 5ft 8in. Two things he hadn't done before getting locked up were exercise or read books, but somehow my book pulled him in and he finished it in two days.

When Ben first went to prison, he rowed a little bit, but after reading my book he decided to really do something with his exercise and started getting interested in the SkiErg. As his fitness started to improve, he moved to HMP Featherstone and they gave him a gym orderly job, where his fitness went to the next level. He was there for about seven months and then got moved to HMP Sudbury, where he got talking to a prison officer called Mark Sherriff, who, coincidentally, was with me when I did the world's longest continuous row, for 45 hours.

Mark is a PE instructor and asked Ben if he'd be interested in doing some work down at the gym. Ben said, 'Yes please.' Mark then started setting Ben challenges, and in December 2024 he said, 'I want you to do a challenge for me to raise money for charity,' and Ben said, 'Okay.' It was supposed to be 147,000 metres throughout the month on a SkiErg, but when Ben told him he thought it was easy, Mark said, 'Why don't you try doing a marathon or half marathon.' Ben did that, and Mark then said, 'Why don't you stay on there for three hours and see what you can do.' Ben did that, and similar to what Darren said to me, Mark said to Ben, 'You know there's records out there for the SkiErg?' and Ben said, 'No. I haven't got a clue.'

Mark then started telling Ben about me, and Ben said, 'I've read his book.' Mark said, 'I think you should go for 100,000 metres.' Ben replied, a bit shocked, 'Nonstop? You're being daft. I'd never be able to do that.' Mark suggested, 'We'll do a training plan and see what you can do.'

On 28 January 2025, Ben didn't plan to break any records, it just happened. He was supposed to go for five hours, see how far he could go, but after the five hours he said, 'I feel alright. Can I carry on?' Mark managed to sort it out with security and Ben went for it. Like when I was doing my rowing records, nutrition-wise you're not allowed things like carbo gels, so he ended up having a flapjack, Bakewell tart, easy-peel oranges, wine gums and some jelly babies. He had lads feeding him from behind, who were coming in and out of the gym, as he didn't stop. Even when he was thirsty, he ended up doing the SkiErg one-handed while having a drink.

The British record for the 100,000 metres was seven hours 22 minutes and 51 seconds, but he smashed it and become the new record holder on the Concept 2 SkiErg machine, in 7 hours one minute and 58 seconds. Not only that, he raised £1,000 for charity in the process. He didn't sleep for two days, because his body was in bits and it took him a few weeks to come to grips with what he'd done, but as he started walking around the prison, people kept saying, 'Well done, mate. Congratulations on doing that.' That's when it started to kick in. That experience changed his physical and mental health focus, and ultimately his path of rehabilitation. Ben's experience has now started a new circle of positivity and, when he's in the prison gym, other prisoners will come up to him and ask him to help design a fitness programme for them or just get general fitness tips.

So, in answer to the chapter title – whenever I speak with people, do podcasts or interviews and they ask, 'What ever happened to that prison officer who encouraged you on the rowing machine in prison? You know, the bloke who was looking over your shoulder inspiring you to break records.' I tell them with a big smile, 'I'm still very close friends with him.'

'I originally wanted to be a professional boxer. I was based in north London and was part of the Gloves Not Gunz charity, based in south London, run by the founder, the late Adam Ballard. John was an ambassador of the charity and I'd connected with him on social media, but I'd never met him in real life at that point.

'Then we met at a boxing meet and it was kind of hi and bye, see you next time. Then I saw some of the boys from Croydon Amateur Boxing Club share this opportunity on social media, called the Alpine Run Project. I applied and was asked to go up to the Nike headquarters. When I got up there, I saw Adam and I was, like, "What are you doing here?" I found out that he had put in a good word to John and Jasper. I thought to myself, "Adam. You don't really know me. Why would you do that?" That was such an amazing moment.

'I started running in year one of the Alpine Run Project in 2023 and, I'll be honest, I didn't even know what trail running was. However, I saw this opportunity to travel and to work with big brands in marketing and thought, "If I prove myself, this could be a way in." I think running was a vehicle to help me pursue what I wanted to do. I was also quite overweight, so it helped in that aspect. However, the biggest thing for me was that it taught me you have to create your opportunities in life. Don't wait around. Make it happen. The project has also given me work opportunities in a paid capacity. Four months after I graduated from the programme, in December of 2023 I started working for Nike with their marketing team in London. Since then, I now work freelance for seven different companies, but the reason I can do that is because of the confidence I've been able to build up. As John always says, 'If an opportunity comes to you, just take it. Even if you don't know how to do it, you can work it our yourself and learn afterwards.' That's become my mindset now. Give everything a hundred per cent, keep an open mind and keep learning along the way.

'One of the biggest things I've learned from John is creating a positive mindset to find solutions. For example – I had my A Levels coming up and I was thinking, "What happens if it goes wrong? Really bad thing could happen. Maybe I can't get into uni next year." But then, I think, *John was stuck in a prison cell and if he managed to get to where he is, I can get through this.* I know it's not a linear journey for everyone and not everyone can get themselves out, but John's helped to create that mindset that if, for example, I didn't do as well as I wanted to in my A levels, what's the worst that could happen? It's fine. It's human nature. We'll get ourselves out of that situation. He's helped me to become very solution orientated. I go after what I want to do in life and create that path to make it happen.

'I would totally recommend any young person between 16 and 23 to get involved with the Alpine Run. You lose weight and mentally become clearer, but running can be a vehicle to whatever you want to do. Alpine Run Project brings creative industries and sport together. Overall, it teaches you to become your best self. Show up and give your hundred per cent. It can unlock so many opportunities and you don't have to be a runner to join. Trail running is just the vehicle to get you to be where you want to in life.

'In terms of social media, our audience isn't just young people. There are people in the sports industry who makes comments about what a great event this is and how influential it is. The real power comes from those individuals on the project who take to social media. They say how it changed their lives and why. When you see a video of John taking these young people on a training camp, these young people could have never had the opportunity to go to somewhere like Girona or the Alps. I'm one of those people.'

—Marek Sthalekar

Chapter 19

Cannes I Kick It?

'Opportunity knocks at any time in life and everybody should answer that door when it does. Go for it!'

—Amanda Redman

IN JUNE 2025, there was an event in Cannes called Sport Beach. Every single major global sports brand was represented there by a CEO, CFO or similar. I'm talking top-of-the-tree businesses and they ship in some of the best athletes in the world, such as Noah Lyles, Mo Farah and Roger Federer, you name it.

The organisers asked me to speak, and I said, 'I'll do it, but I want one of the kids from the Alpine Run Project to come with me.' They had to email all these people in New York because you can't just rock up to this event. Getting a ticket for the four days costs £1,500, plus you've got to send in your LinkedIn profile, the position you hold in that company, why you want to be there and what you are hoping to get out of it. You've got all these global CEOs and they want to make sure the right people are there with all these global athletes.

You have to remember, they were paying for me to fly business class, putting me up in a five-star hotel, so I wasn't really expecting them to agree … but they did! They said I would have to cover my own travel, but that was fine. I would have rather gifted Marek the opportunity to come out, because he would get the most out of it. Although I was really looking forward to telling Marek about the opportunity, I was also aware that he was a student and needed to prioritise what was best for him.

I called him up and explained about the event and that all the biggest names in the world of sport would be coming together in an industry he wanted to progress in. I said, 'It's like the pinnacle opportunity if you want to pursue something like this in life, and a great opportunity to take inspiration from business and sportspeople, their creativity and how it all comes together.' I then added, 'Listen, I know you have an A level on the Thursday and this event is on the Tuesday, so I have to remind you that your exams are your priority. If this event could have an effect on your results, then you shouldn't come. There will always be another event.'

He asked me loads of questions and I mentioned about some of the companies and athletes that would be attending, plus we would be running with Mo Farah and the CEO of Strava. Marek took what I said on board, and said, 'It's more about what I can prove to myself. I've stayed committed on what I wanted to do this summer, doubling down on everything. For me, this event in Cannes and the opportunities it brings could be more important than any academic qualification. Maybe I'll be wrong in the future, but I'll learn that way.' I said, 'That day in Cannes will be here and gone, so it's about maximising the potential in that time, but also not ignoring the months and years of hard work it took to get you to the point of taking an exam.' He nodded.

Shortly after, I put Marek in touch with the travel people, who organised flights, and he messaged me and said, 'Mate! I can't believe it. They're flying me out business class. And they've attached the invoice. It says two grand!' Marek's a lovely kid, and I told him that. If he wasn't the person he is, he wouldn't have gone to Cannes. He's a good person, has a good heart and wants to help other people, and everyone will see that throughout his life. That experience in Cannes is something that will lift him for the rest of his life, and that brings me more joy than the fact that I was going.

Unfortunately for Marek, he's growing up in a generation where many kids think that fame and influence is getting a blue tick on social media and having lots of followers. Before the event, I said to him, 'It goes back to Adam Ballard at Gloves Not Gunz. In life, the people with real influence you will hardly know them. If you just do the right things in life, people will see you doing the right things for the right reasons and doors will open for you. They will be the people in the shadows, the people like the David Deins of this world, they're the ones with influence, not the players. When you come down to Cannes, for instance, that environment – that's influence. These people working in these corporations, doing what they do to help future generations, they're the ones that can really create that sense of social change and can have an impact on thousands and millions of people's lives. When you are in that room, you've got to network and converse with them, but also remember, if you do manage to create these opportunities, then you have to give back. You have to help other people. One day you'll be in the situation I'm in. You need to tap into that, not the person on Instagram who's an influencer. Not looking through that prism of how many Instagram followers you have, how many views your content gets.

'When Adam passed away in early 2025, he had a massive influence and impact on your life and got you to apply for the Alpine Run. Me and Adam had an amazing relationship and, when Adam died, I messaged you and said, "Just remember one thing. Adam was a real influencer. He had real influence in that community and he genuinely cared about the people who he was helping." Remember that. He wasn't doing it because the byproduct was that he was getting something out of it. He was doing it because he wanted to help, and he influenced the lives of thousands of kids in that community. That's what influence is.'

Thankfully, Marek really got it and from the get-go he was ready to put all that into practice as he embarked on this trip to Cannes.

I made my own way to Cannes and got there on the Sunday. I picked up all the passes, for myself, Marek, Stephen Manderson (aka Professor Green) and Will Howe. Will works for Sidekick, which is more a traditional creative agency, and they joined the Stagwell network in 2024. He's a super-nice guy with a great energy about him and was genuinely very passionate about what the Alpine Run Project was trying to achieve. Incredibly, there was an organic tie-in, as his cousin set up Football Beyond Borders with Jasper around 2011, and Will had already been lending his support to them for a while. Then when Will started to read about the Alpine Run Project on LinkedIn, through Football Beyond Borders, he thought, *That's an area I really want to get involved in*. He watched the first documentary that was made and it turns out he knew a couple of the guys who had produced that.

Once I'd picked the passes up, a lady called Fiona, who works for Stagwell, said, 'Would you like to come for a drink for a catch-up?' We'd only done Zoom calls up to this point. Fiona is a down-to-earth, easy-going person and it was interesting to hear how she hadn't taken the traditional path into her job in Stagwell. She used to work in Thailand doing deep-sea diving photography for tourists, which was a business that she and her husband ran from one of the islands. Then she decided she wanted a new challenge, went to London and got introduced to someone who then introduced her to someone at Stagwell, and she got the job.

That Sunday night I was invited to go out with the Stagwell team before the events started on the Monday, to network before the madness of Sport Beach started. These guys were mainly from New York and worked for a big marketing agency. Lovely people, and we had some interesting conversations about philosophy in life and how we all see it, where I came from and where they came from. I then went back to the villa where we were staying. It was the first time I'd been there. I wasn't expecting anything special, maybe just a nice little place out of town, but when I got there I was blown away. It was an amazing villa in the hills, which would have easily been worth €5 million, with a massive swimming pool, a dolphin design on the tiles at the bottom of the pool and that whole terracotta design, which you would associate with the south of France. It's a weird one, though, because years ago that was my life to a degree, and I would have been overly impressed, because of the lifestyle I was pursuing. I knew people who had houses like that and I mixed with those people, but my life is so different now. Obviously, there's no way you could not be impressed with the building, but it doesn't do what it used to do for me before.

I was waiting for everyone to arrive, but their flights had been delayed, so I thought, *Get your head down, you've got a full-on week ahead.* While I was in bed, Marek was having his own adventure. From the airport lounge, he boarded the plane and, being in business class, it was him, then an empty seat in the middle and then this middle-aged American guy. They weren't really talking at the start, but when the announcement came that the plane would be sitting on the runway for the next hour and a half, they looked at each other, rolled their eyes and started laughing. This guy then asked Marek, 'Are you going to the event?' and he replied, 'Sport Beach?' This guy said, 'Yes. That's the one.'

Marek was now interested to know what this guy did. It turned out he came from San Francisco and managed Adobe's products. He explained that he managed the team that sold the products to the clients and he shared some stories with Marek. Not one to miss an opportunity, Marek asked, 'How could I work in these circles?' He then shared some challenges he'd been working on and how he'd overcome them. The guy warmed to Marek and gave him some great advice for the future. That one-and-a-half-hour delay was a blessing in disguise, plus an hour-and-a-half flight, which gave Marek three hours of very productive networking. Shortly before landing, this guy said, 'We've just launched this product called Adobe Express, and we would like to hear your thoughts on it. Let's catch up in Cannes.' As you can imagine, Marek was made up. Then, to top it off, Marek, Will and Stephen jumped into a flash black van with darkened windows, with Marek sat next to Stephen. Just to make sure they made their mark, when they arrived around 1am, they had a swim in the pool, set the alarm off, then went to bed.

In the morning, it was nice having a catch-up with Marek, and it was amazing to have him in that environment with me and to share this experience with him. The four of us got on so well, which is not always the case when you put a group of individuals together who don't all know each other. Sometimes when you go to these types of events you can easily find yourself exhausted, because you're trying to burn the candle at both ends, but that week the playing field was levelled. We had myself as an athlete, a young person in Marek, a rapper who is now teetotal, and Will, who doesn't particularly drink. It felt so energising being around these guys. It was like hanging out with three best mates and felt like a holiday, as much as it was work.

One of the highlights was seeing Stephen showing Marek how to cook a steak. He'd never cooked a steak before in his life and Stephen is really into his cooking. That's what it's about. It's those little life moments that allow people to grow. I have to say a few words about Stephen/Professor Green. I can't speak highly of him enough. A very genuine guy who is very giving with his time. We had quite a few deep, philosophical conversations and talked about the environments we grew up in and how the perception of weakness was prevalent, with crime and gangs, and how that can affect you later on in life. He was also very open on his mental health and stuff. I haven't heard anyone say a bad word about him.

As far as the event goes, I'll be honest, it's not something I love doing because I find these things quite draining. I'm kind of a social introvert/extrovert. I can switch it on, but then I get drained with the one-on-one stuff. I always have to remind myself, *People might not always remember what you've said to them, but they will always remember how you make them feel*, so I always want to genuinely make people feel like they've been listened to and heard, and come away with a positive experience of interacting with me.

We got picked up on that first day in the morning, in a van, and drove to the event. It was like an extension of the Cannes Film Festival, and when walking down the promenade there was a big Google Beach sign, Snapchat, a big hotel behind us with LinkedIn, Adobe, Netflix, Meta and X. That gave you a sense of the magnitude of the event and the amount of money that had gone into it. Then when you took a look at the rota and saw the likes of Serena Willams talking, all these NBA and NFL players, loads of massive actors and actresses such as Reese Witherspoon, then there's 50 Cent rapping. It was a lot to take in. It was impressive in the scale of it all, but for me the big thing was having Marek there. That paid testament to what I was trying to achieve.

When we got there that morning and went into Sport Beach for the first time, we were in a room with about 70 people, with all these big brands from across the world. The lady sitting next to me was from Apple; then there was a guy sitting close to me called Michael Sugar, who is a big-name American film and television producer. There was an interview going on with a gymnast and an NFL player, and they were talking about mental health and the coping strategies they use to help them not fall into a big, deep black hole. Really interesting people.

Once that was done, we went downstairs and there was a big open space, which had a basketball court and a big stage, where the athletes would go on stage to speak. It wasn't how I thought it was going to be. It was all very light-hearted and informal, not like so many other events I'd been to in the past where everyone is chucking business cards around from the start. It was much more fun than I anticipated, but that also had something to do with the group I was with – Helen, Fiona, Marek, Professor Green and Will. They really understood what I stood for and they were really generous with their time to Marek, which I thought was beautiful, especially as they had concerns in advance that Marek would be overwhelmed by the event, due to the fact that he was the youngest person there by a country mile. Well, after speaking with him, that put their minds at rest.

The highlight of Monday morning was running with Sir Mo Farah and getting him to mention the Alpine Run to millions of followers. Here's what happened. I was talking to Mo Farah's agent, James, and was meant to do a podcast with Mo, but, as you can imagine, his schedule was crazy, doing runs and accepting a few awards. James said, 'Let's see if we can get something in, even though it might be difficult,' which it was. Helen and Fiona from Stagwell said, 'This run is happening anyway, so come along and take part in the event and then there might be opportunities to get some content for Alpine Run.' I said, 'Great!' Marek was excited, to say the least.

It was a really hot day, but we all did a three-mile run with Mo, and then Mo went off by himself at one point to film a little piece, just so he could run really fast for the media. We then circled back, and James Mitchell got some images of me, Mo and Marek along the beach. Then we came back. Marek said to Mo, 'I'm part of the Alpine Run Project with John McAvoy, Nike,' and so on, and Mo said he was more than happy to speak to the camera and give the participants a best of luck message going into races in the summer.

When you get someone like Mo Farah, one of the biggest Nike athletes in the world, promoting Alpine Run, that doesn't get lost on Nike senior leadership people. Marek was amazing that morning, doing what he did with the content and the professionalism he showed speaking with a mega name like Mo Farah. He also got to meet Olympic sprint champion Noah Lyles, who had not long before done a talk on mindsets in the world of sport. Will Howe got a picture of them, but Marek didn't really recognise Noah at first. He'd just walked off the stage and into the public, and normally at an event where Noah Lyles speaks, you'd never get to be next to him, he's simply whisked off stage. However, because this event was so exclusive, the agencies and managers didn't mind them interacting with the attendees. Obviously, there was security, but no heavy restrictions. He was playing basketball with people from the crowd and Marek managed to get a quick picture and chat with him before he went to get some food.

As far as my session goes, I was meant to be speaking on stage with Professor Green on the Thursday, but because I had to leave on the Tuesday they moved the schedule around. Professor Green still did his event on the Thursday and then I did the dinner, where there were the likes of the CEO of the National Lottery, people from Rolex and Cartier and a guy from Dubai, who was very interested to get the Alpine Run out to the Middle East. More about that later.

So, my position had moved from me talking on stage to talking at the dinners instead, and meeting all these different brands and agencies. It was great networking, standing in front of all these incredible people, and I'm confident we can get several of them involved with Alpine Run in the future. There's also that knock-on effect of speaking to agencies, who then speak to other agencies, which could also help plug our young people into different job opportunities. It was genuinely a wonderful event, and when Monday finished I was seriously tempted to stay on until the Thursday, but I had to get back because I was racing the next Sunday.

As we were getting ready to go our separate ways, Marek wrapped up his last bit of networking on the Tuesday. Following on from the conversation he had with the guy from Adobe on the plane, Marek was invited to the hotel where the Adobe guys were staying, to chat with the vice-president of Adobe Express about what he thought about the program. Marek gave his views and thoughts, but he didn't want to leave it there. He'd developed this relationship with two senior people at Adobe and thought it would be a shame if he didn't at least try to see if there was anything he could do with them after.

Marek edited the Mo Farah video using their product and sent them a deck after the event and a thank-you message. He also added what he thought he could bring to the team if given the opportunity. In the meantime, two days after that meeting with Adobe, he sat his A level and in his own words straight after, 'It was as tough as I expected it to be. It perhaps didn't go as well as I'd hoped, but it was a calculated risk and I don't regret it at all.' Thankfully, a couple of months later, Marek got his results and did really well with all three of his A levels, and as a result of that chat with the guy on the plane from Heathrow to Cannes, he's now an ambassador for Adobe Express. All in all, a productive event.

Chapter 20

Wake-Up Call

'The past is never the past. It is always present. And you better reckon with it in your life and in your daily experience, or it will get you. It will get you really bad.'

—Bruce Springsteen

AT THE beginning of this book we had Edgar talking about how Nike took me on board in 2017, and here we are now in 2026, talking about a beautiful full circle with Nike as we discuss their support for me and the Alpine Run Project into the future. However, the ten weeks leading up to these meetings with Nike at the end of 2025 were physically the worst of my life. Here's what happened.

On Thursday, 28 August 2025, a couple of days after the Alpine Run Project runners completed the UTMB YCC race, I ran the OCC, which was 57km, with an elevation gain of over 3,500m. As I started running into Chamonix town centre for the last kilometre, there were some of the guys from the Alpine Run cheering me, but I was so zoned out because I'd only taken on about half the calories I should have for a race that long, simply because I couldn't keep anything down and kept vomiting. I was on the limit of completely imploding and running out of energy, so my mind was set on crossing the line at all costs.

I was so fatigued that I could kind of realise people were around me, then with about 300 metres to go, I could sense some of the guys from the Alpine Run were running with me to the finish line, going past all the bars and restaurants as everyone was clapping and cheering and the cowbells were going. You run past the statue of the two climbers looking up to Mont Blanc, then you start to hit the blue carpet for the final bit, and that's when the hairs on your neck go up.

With about 50 metres to go, as my guys from the Alpine Run were shouting, 'Let's go, John,' I couldn't enjoy it because I was fucked. I looked up and saw the other kids at the finish line. I got to the end and almost collapsed with exhaustion. Although I couldn't fully appreciate it right after, that was probably the best moment of my life. My friend Lisa said to me, 'Just think. Four years ago you came here all on your own, and look at you now. You've got 50 kids crossing the line with you and look at what you've done for them.'

That night, I watched the video and it was amazing. I lost count of the number of people who saw it and said that they'd got emotional watching it, which made me very proud. I appreciated the significance of it and it was an amazing moment for the project and the kids.

I got back to Alpe d'Huez on the Saturday, and when I woke up Sunday morning my body was drenched in sweat. I was badly fatigued, so I rested for the remainder of the day and thought, *Maybe you haven't got over that cold you had before the race.* Then on the Monday I went out to do a run and my heart rate went from about 48 beats a minute up to 160 within about 90 seconds. I thought my heart rate monitor strap wasn't working properly so removed it, but that made no difference. I did the same thing again the day after and went for an easy run, but again, bang, my heart rate went through the roof.

The next day I decided to have a lighter one and did some stuff on the rowing machine, but the same issue happened with my heartbeat flying high up, so I decided not to train for the rest of that week. As my pulse started to settle down again, I jumped on a rowing machine the week after and everything seemed stable, but when I went out on the bike something started to go wrong with my stomach. I was getting excruciating cramps and feeling really sick, and thought, *It's just a stomach bug. Suck it up.* I carried on training, then the following week the madness started.

I went for an easy 60-minute run in the valley where I live, and about 35 minutes into it, on the way back, I had this feeling of blowing up. I'd bonked. Completely out of energy. I was thinking, *What the fuck is wrong with me?* It was like I was at the back end of an Ironman after about nine hours. I walked back to the car and blamed it on not eating properly the night before. It was beyond fatigue, though. It was like someone had put the accelerator down full tilt on me and the engine was revving up but not coming down.

I thought I could get over it by tailoring my training, so brought the volume and intensity down, and just stuck to maintenance work, because I still intended to do the UTMB in Nice in September and the one in Sweden in October. I thought I could just ride off the back of the stamina from the UTMB in Chamonix and get through this, but that wasn't going to happen.

In order to help my body recover, I decided to go to stay at my friend's house in the south of France for four days, to get away from altitude, and I also pulled out of the UTMB Nice, with the intention of focusing on Sweden in October. I went out on my bike, but after about an hour still felt like I was bonking, was getting major headaches and sleeping for nine hours, but felt like I was sleeping for five minutes, because when I woke up I felt like I had a constant hangover, but without actually drinking alcohol.

I decided to go back to Chamonix and get some bloods done, because I thought I might be iron deficient. I went to the blood lab, had all my bloods taken and they all came back clear, which made me even more confused. My low white blood cell count was put down to the virus I had picked up in Chamonix during the time of the UTMB, so I thought, *Okay. You've not recovered properly, but you can manage your way out of this.* Stupidly, I kept training.

I was still all set to go to Sweden and set off about 6am after breakfast, but felt really groggy. I stopped along the way and grabbed a coffee in Switzerland, then a couple of hours later I was about two and a half hours from Hamburg and grabbed some food in one of those petrol station laybys. As I was there, my left hand and left side of my face went numb. I thought I was having a heart attack, and I was the only one in this layby. I was there for 30 minutes and I said to myself, 'You are not having a heart attack, but whatever is going on, get in the car, get to Hamburg and at least you are in a city and there's going to be people about.'

I got to Hamburg, went straight to the hotel, jumped into bed and slept for ten hours. I woke up next morning and thought, *You're done, mate.* I got in touch with Paul Gurney from BecomingX, sending him an email explaining that I wouldn't be able to come up for the World's Deepest Marathon (more about that event later). I then decided to get back to the UK, because I'd be able to get the medical treatment I wanted a lot quicker.

I drove from Hamburg to Amsterdam, got on the night ferry, slept, landed at Harwich, drove straight to Putney to stay with a mate and then from there to Chiswick and had my full blood panels done, ECG, everything. All the bloods came back absolutely fine, which again was very annoying. I then went to see a sports medicine doctor and it turned out I was a classic textbook case. You get a virus, you have a lag for about three or four weeks and then that virus, in my case, deregulated my autonomic nervous system, which controls all of your body's involuntary functions that you don't think about, like your brain, liver, kidneys, digestion, breathing, heart rate, etc. In brief, my autonomic nervous system was fucked. For example, eating food wasn't a problem, but my body wasn't able to efficiently process it, to deliver it to the vital organs.

I explained to the doctor about my last year, in terms of my own exercise, what I'd been organising, and the fact was I'd been ill in 2025 more than I'd been my entire life. I asked whether what had happened might have also been stress from all the projects I'd been juggling, and he said, no, it was down to the viral infection. However, he did say that everything together was like death by a thousand cuts throughout the year. I had a kidney infection in January 2025, which lasted seven weeks, then came out of that, got a viral infection and wasn't giving my body a break. I think I'd finally realised I wasn't bomb-proof, and since then value my health as the most precious thing on this Earth.

However, as they say, the show must go on, and the next few weeks was stacked, to put it mildly.

'I used to be a cheerleader and had done that most of my life, but just before the pandemic started, I decided to do a parkrun with my friend. When we went into lockdown I was doing 3km here and there and then when we came out of lockdown I carried on running, but basically to help with my cheerleading, but it was never more than 10km. Then in 2023 I saw the Alpine Project on someone's random story on Instagram and I thought, "*Oh. That looks cool. I've always wanted to go to the mountains.*"

'In the years before, I had friends at school, but they were just friends because we were in school together. We didn't really have anything in common and I didn't really agree with a lot of the things they enjoyed. I wanted to find more people that I had stuff in common with, like travelling and running. So, I got on the project and got way more obsessed with running and quit cheerleading after the first year of the project.

'From one year to the next I was concerned about the project not having the same vibe of people, because in the first year everyone was so positive and so spontaneous. I was concerned it wouldn't be the same the year after, but I think the Alpine Run Project attracts the right people. Even though everyone is so different and has different stories, it attracts people who are willing to open up and put themselves in vulnerable situations. They just know the project is completely non-judgemental and they instantly feel confident coming into it.

'My dad passed away during lockdown and the project came at a good time, because it gave me such a positive focus to aim for. I realised there's no way I was not going to be part of it moving forward and decided to become more involved with the Alpine Run Project. I've been through it from the start and I'm in a position to help the other young people on it. In 2025 I applied to be a project ambassador, and part of that role was to be a race coordinator, helping people sort out entries for the races, organise their travel and webinars, and be there for anyone who had questions or needed help.

'John McAvoy has introduced me to so many people that have shown me what can be done with sport and he's exposed me to so many new amazing places. Everyone can take something from the project. You might not be the biggest fan of trail running but just getting outside and realising that even if you live in a city, you can still get the train to somewhere which has open spaces, like the Peak District. People like me might fall in love with trail running and want to get better at it, some people might see job opportunities, all because of the project. The network is so big within the project that somebody will be able to tell you about somebody and will help to give you the position you are after. I'd go as far as saying that this project can change lives. It's certainly changed mine.'

—Eleana Matos

With Ian Wright at Wembley Stadium for the Twinning Project launch, 2018

At Oudenaarde Prison with Imogen and the prison governor

With Paul Gurney at the House of Lords

With actor Joe Cole and Olympic rowers, Jess Eddie and Moe Sbihi, at an Open Doors talk, in a London school

With Zeb, from the Idris Elba show, taking him to Chelsea FC for his first football match

With the inspirational David Smith MBE, at UTMB 2025

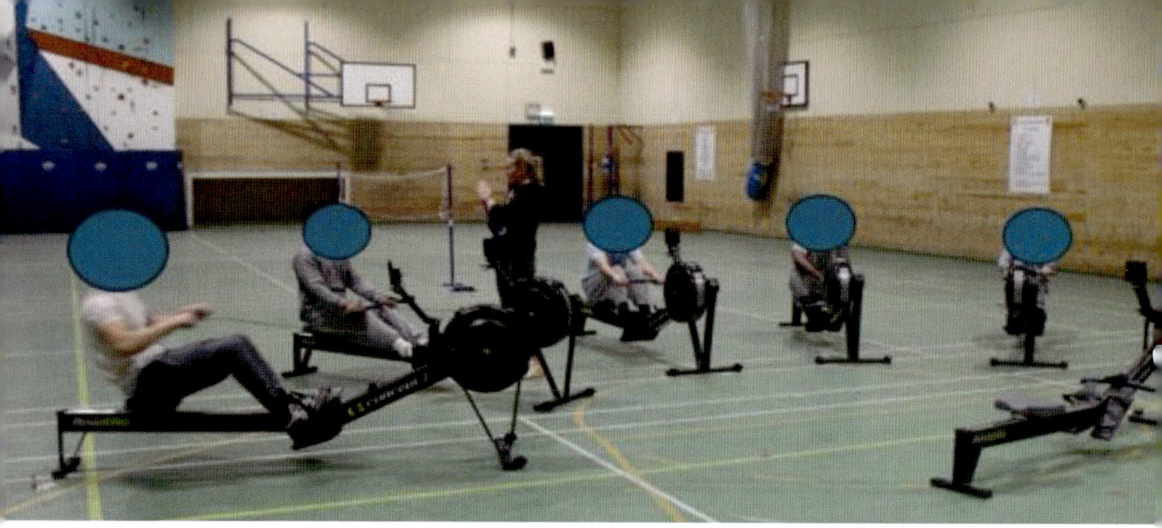

Imogen Walsh delivering Boats Not Bars

With Edgar at Nike HQ Hilversum, pitching the idea of the Alpine Run Project

Riding with Geraint Thomas 2022

UTMB 2025 – with the Alpine Run Project

With Idris Elba on set

With Jasper at the House of Lords at a UK Active event in 2018

Signing away my Life Licence and gaining my freedom in 2019

At a JD Sports event with Toby Hunter, Kane Mousah, Darren Davis and a JD exec

With Mo Farah at Sport Beach, Cannes (Photo Credit James Mitchell)

Marek and Noah Lyles, Sport Beach, Cannes

With Stephen Manderson, AKA Professor Green, Will Howe and James Mitchell

'I first briefly met John when I moved back to Europe with Nike, having spent a few years over in Nike World Headquarters, in Oregon, USA. This was a couple of years after John signed his first Nike athlete contract in 2017. I had heard from team-mates and friends in Nike Europe about John, his personal story and at that point what he was doing as an individual athlete.

'At that time, there were Nike leaders who were working closely with John and had got to know him in the way that I do today, and had the belief in John and his vision for Alpine Run Project. I am incredibly grateful to those in Nike before me or who had that belief in John and the project. I am immensely grateful and proud to be able to carry this forward and support John and the Alpine Run Project to continue to build from strength to strength.

'I then met John properly in 2023, when ARP was off the ground. What I realised instantly when I first met John, to what is so true today, is this is not about John. When he talks, he only talks about the projects; when he talks, he only talks about the kids; and when he talks about changing lives, it's the lives of others.

'His personal story is one that is quite incredible, one of redemption, one of strength, and one of lessons. But all of this he channels into making others better and changing lives for others. He is one of the most selfless, humble and caring people I've met. Someone who truly embodies the athlete mindset and so firmly believes in how the sport has the power to change lives.

'As the VP/GM of Nike in EMEA, the thing I am most passionate about is sport. Sport is full of incredible stories of transformation, redemption, comebacks. Sport writes stories that scriptwriters couldn't, and when you see this come to life it's magnificent. Individual wins, team wins, but none of those are as powerful as when sport gets to transform lives. And this is what is so powerful about John's personal story, and that he took that personal lesson, a life saved and changed by sport, then dedicated his time as an athlete and a human, and created Alpine Run Project with the mission and vision to get hundreds and thousands of kids from the streets, to the outdoors, into trail running, into the wild and build a lifelong relationship with sport.

'This aligns so incredibly to the values of the Nike brand and so closely to a couple of things that Nike, and me as an individual, believe in to our core. That if you have a body, you are an athlete, and that sport has the power to change the world. With Alpine Run Project, that is what John and the team are doing, and we are very proud to be a part of that.'

—Chris Thornton
VP/GM for Nike Brand EMEA

Chapter 21

The Journey Continues

I WAS in the UK, going through everything with the doctors with blood tests and all that for this post-viral fatigue, but I still had to go to the Netherlands, to the Nike HQ in Hilversum, to discuss the futures of the Alpine Run Project and my own personal contract renewal with Nike.

I decided to get the night ferry so I could get some sleep and feel a bit recharged when I got to the offices. On 2 November 2025, I went down to Harwich at 8pm to get the 10pm ferry, took my dinner with me, went straight to my cabin, went to sleep before the ferry departed, then woke up in the morning, just as we were pulling into the dock in the Netherlands.

Whenever I go to the Netherlands, it's always a medley of emotions, because my best friend died there and all those memories from many years ago when I was doing bad stuff, being surrounded by hundreds of thousands of pounds in 500 euro notes, whereas these days my travels that way are all very positive and that's because of my relationship with Nike.

I got to Hilversum and went straight to the hotel and chilled all day, then met up with my old mate Toby and had a nice catch-up. Jasper was already over at Hilversum, as he'd been doing meetings the day before, and that evening I went out for dinner with Jasper, Toby and another lad from Youth Beyond Borders. We were discussing the meeting that was happening the next day and how we hoped it would play out, then I went back to the hotel very early and had a long sleep.

I woke up, felt semi-fresh, had breakfast and then I had a bit of a turn when I got into my taxi. Robert, the cab driver who picked me up for my first-ever trip to the Netherlands, was the same person who picked me up this time, which was a lovely reconnection. We had a hug and started chatting, but when I sat down I felt whacked. I was sat in the back with Jasper and I said to him, 'Mate, if I zone out in the meeting, you're going to have to pick it up for me.' It wasn't just one meeting, though, it was a day of meetings.

We went to the office, picked up our passes and got to the meeting room 15 minutes early to set up and make sure all the tech was working. There was the general manager of Nike, the vice-president, the head of ACG (All Conditions Gear), head of global comms, you name it. Basically, all the senior leadership team at Nike Europe, with me and Jasper presenting the vision of the Alpine Run.

Chris Thornton, the VP/GM at Nike Europe, who is an absolutely lovely lad from Newcastle, overheard that I felt like shit and said, 'I'll cancel the meeting.' I said, 'No, let's go ahead, but I just wanted to warn you, if I zone out and do the UFC Tapout, Jasper's going to have to pick it up.'

Here we were in the meeting, which went on for about an hour, and I led on it, while Jasper frameworked it in, with regards to how the project was going to be delivered. Then at the end of the meeting, Chris stood up and pointed towards the screen and he said, 'It's not *if* we do it, it's *how* we do it,' which was obviously amazing. It hadn't been signed off at that point, but that was a massive step in the right direction.

I got through that meeting, had lunch and went to the next one. By the time we were done that day, I went back to the hotel and I was fucked. My brain was going at a million miles an hour and I had this fluttering sensation in my chest, which it turns out was tachycardia, which meant my heart was going at over 100 beats per minute as I was sat there doing nothing. At a later date, I had an echocardiogram and my heart was fine; it was just down to my nervous system again.

The day after, I had to have a meeting with the Nike running brand team, and by now I felt better, mainly because the amount of pressure from that first meeting to deliver it was now over. After that, I had a meeting with sports marketing, who are the guys who look after the athletes. There was another Chris, again a lovely guy, and he wanted 30 minutes with me before writing me a contract. He needed to understand where Nike saw me within the brand for the next four years, my importance to the business and the value I added.

We discussed my relationship with Nike and what worked and didn't work. I explained that I wasn't like some of these football players who turned up once or twice a year to a project and they take pictures of them; instead, I was actively leading on this stuff, running it and supporting anyone who needed it all year round. Chris acknowledged that. Then the next day we were working with Nike's ACG team in a two-hour meeting. They were going to be working on the Alpine Run Project and were basically deciding its future.

The meeting was very productive and it was amazing to know the project was going to be taken on by Nike and that we would be of strategic importance for them in future, which would secure the project for a long time. Not to mention the opportunities it would provide for the kids with Nike directly in the future. With everything in place, there was nothing more I could do, except head back to London for my next meetings.

***

When the Alpine Run was first created, it was never intended to be a performance project, but in that first year, we had two young people, Eleana and David, who stood out. Eleana won the YCC at UTMB 2022 and David was a phenomenal runner. People at Nike obviously saw their potential to become trail runners and there was a conversation around creating a pathway for those more talented athletes to potentially one day become fully fledged Nike athletes.

Nike decided to bring Sports Shoes in, a retail partner of theirs, and this would act like a stepping stone. If they keep on progressing, then eventually they could migrate across to a Nike contract. Unfortunately, David decided he wanted to focus on his track running and didn't take up the opportunity, which is fair enough as this was trail running, but Eleana took the opportunity with both hands.

When Sports Shoes officially became a partner of Alpine Run Project, I got in touch with them and said, 'There's some other runners on the project this year who are really talented. Could we bring some more on board with Eleana?' Gavin, who worked in marketing at Sports Shoes, said, 'Yes. We've got a budget for three young people.' I then picked Charlotte Rawstron and Taylor-Von Massey to accompany Eleana as the three Nike/Sports Shoes ambassadors.

Those contracts they signed that morning put them on the path to becoming professional runners. In addition to their natural ability, this contract provided them with a small kitty of money and some products to help them with their racing journey. Obviously, they are still young and developing, and at that age you can have all the talent in the world, but there's so many other components that are needed to make you a success as an athlete. You need the right mindset, support structure, the right coach, etc., but this contract opened doors for them.

Back to November 2025. On the morning of the 7th, I headed back to London and went into the Nike offices with Eleana, Charlotte and Taylor, to get their contracts signed with Sports Shoes. It was a Sports Shoes/Nike ambassadorial contract, being run by the Sports Shoes team, but with Nike affiliated to it. The contracts would then be officially announced at the Alpine Run Project 2025 graduation later that night at this plush Samsung office, near Kings Cross, so, in the meantime, I went back to Putney to chill out for a few hours and recharge.

When I got to Kings Cross that evening, it was like a sensory overload as hundreds of people were standing around talking. It was all down to this post-viral fatigue. I'll be honest, if it wasn't for the kids, I wouldn't have gone up. I actually pulled out of 95 per cent of all the plans I had for when I got back to the UK, including some massive podcasts and corporate events. The minute I walked through the door, it hit me like a ton of bricks and I had to pull the project manager aside and say, 'I'm not going to be able to get up and do any speaking tonight.' She gently asked, 'Could you not even say a few lines?' I said, 'Absolutely not. I don't feel well enough to do it. I probably shouldn't even be here.' I then turned to Jasper and said, 'You're going to have to pick up the baton and do everything tonight.' He asked, 'Are you sure?' I replied, 'I'm absolutely positive.'

When I was sitting at the front of the room, my mate Joe asked, 'How you feeling?' and I replied, 'I feel hot and my brain is buzzing.' It felt like I'd been on the booze and drugs, I was that spaced out. When the kids came out on stage, it was heartwarming to listen to, but I just wasn't present. I ended up by getting on stage for about 30 seconds, just to apologise that I couldn't do my bit, explained that I wasn't feeling well and then handed it over to Jasper. Immediately afterwards I was out of there and went straight to bed.

***

A few weeks later, on 16 December 2025, we reconvened as a team on the phone and Nike and ACG called to confirm that the Alpine Run Project would be supported until 2029, which was the best news I could have wanted. We are looking at expanding it all over France and, eventually, Spain, UK and the US, ultimately becoming a global pillar of ACG as a top-tier partner. We would be working within Nike's footprint of expansion, being visible in their biggest market spaces.

Two days after getting the news of the Alpine Run contract, I was informed that my personal contract was being extended, which puts me in an elite group of the longest-serving current Nike athletes worldwide. Having worked with them for all these years, I know how rare it is to get a long-term commitment like that, not just for me personally, but taking into account the current economic climate worldwide.

On a personal level, knowing I had the financial security, on both counts, to continue to do what I love made me feel valued and acknowledged, but there was also a big sense of relief. My contract was going to run out within a few months and I didn't know what was going to happen after that, so having that security is incredible. Another thing is knowing that I don't need to stretch myself doing lots of other bits and pieces to generate income, because I have this as my financial backbone. Another thing is pride. I feel very proud of myself for being very true to my values throughout this whole journey and never devaluing myself and giving in to those TV adverts or other sports brand offers. All the decisions I've made since coming out of prison have contributed to me getting this contract extension, even if I had to financially struggle on numerous occasions.

To top off 2025, I was asked to help shape a debate on how to get young people into sport, which I think will be a work in progress for many years to come for me. Nike have got a governmental policy division in the UK now, and they asked me to do a talk to the Commissioner of the Met Police and the commissioners of all of the constabularies across the UK on a big conference call. They also want me to speak at the London Mayor's office and at an event at the House of Commons, around diverting young people away from crime into sport, between the ages of 16 and 19, because there's a real big problem of kids stealing millions and millions of pounds worth of retail products.

It was quite funny, though, because there was about 40 of them on that call and they were mesmerised. On the chat bar on the side, I could see them saying, 'Where do we get his contact details?' Most of them knew my surname and they were really respectful and complimentary, and many of them said how it reminded them of why they came into the job and that it wasn't just about arresting people, but helping the community by preventing it getting to that stage in the first place. I've never claimed to have all the answers, but I think when you put a bunch of like-minded people into a room, amazing things can happen.

'We have a group chat for everyone on the Alpine Run Project and it was advertised on the group for two girls to go and run the World's Deepest Marathon. There's no natural light, you're running with head torches, you've got no music. I thought, "Wow, that sounds really tough, but incredible and when would I ever get the chance to do a world record?" I applied for it and didn't think I'd get it, but if I applied and didn't get it, at least I tried.

'Female participation in trail running is a big thing for me. There's a real lack of diversity in the sport and there was a parallel there with mining, as in there's a lack of women in mining and women are not always taken seriously in a lot of these spaces.

'I got the place and then went over to Alpe d'Huez in July with Eleana, and that's when I really understood that John had made it happen for Toni and I, with Paul Gurney. John said, "I'm so glad you got the place. It's going to open so many doors for you." I ran the London 2025 Marathon in April, and when I finished that I thought, "That was hard, I'm not sure if I'll do another marathon for a while." I would have never thought I would end up doing two in the same year.

'The Marathon was on the BBC news, which is mad. I remember saying to my mother and pointing to the television and saying, "That's me on the news!" I also got asked to go on a running podcast too, which was my very first podcast, and honestly something that I would never have imagined doing before John made this all happen. That marathon has opened so many avenues for me that I didn't see at the time of signing up, because I didn't understand the scale of it. I'm incredibly grateful.'

—Claire-Marie Rozario

'When I was in secondary school I did a bit of sprinting, but never long-distance. Anything more than 200 metres for me was too long. Then when the opportunity came up for the World's Deepest Marathon, it was crazy, because I was telling John that I had only just run my first 5km the week before I joined Alpine Run Project. He was impressed that I was starting this journey from the ground up.

'In the lead-up, we had a couple of calls to hear what my and Claire's concerns were and how he could support us and motivate us on that front, especially as it got closer to the race. The last time we saw him in person before the race was in September 2025 and we met at the Precision Fuel and Hydration HQ in Christchurch, Hampshire, and we were doing heat chamber running, simulating what the conditions could be like in the mine. He was there as well and was also there to give us some last-minute encouragement for the race.

'In terms of applying that achievement to other areas of my life, I've realised that since coming back, I feel I can tackle anything at work, even in my more intense new role. The marathon was the hardest thing I'd ever done. Now, when I go into the office, I know I can succeed, as long as I break things down clearly and approach them calmly, just like I did underground. The race has also given me great confidence that I can actually accomplish things I set my mind to.'

—Toni-Ivana Awofeso

He looked up the existing record for the depth, and thought, *How hard can that be?*

Paul got in touch with a good friend who worked in the mining industry who knew all the CEOs and explained about wanting to organise this race and raise loads of money for charity. Thankfully, he agreed. There were offers from all round the world to host the event, but in the end it was decided that the Garpenberg Zinc Mine in Sweden worked well logistically, which had a potential tunnel to use at 1,119m below sea level. Just to put that into perspective, the Channel Tunnel is 75m at its deepest point, and the world's tallest building, the Burj Khalifa, is 828m.

With the mine in place, he then had to sort out things like getting toilets down there, water, food, lighting, everything. The other bonus for each participant, in addition to taking part in the World's Deepest Marathon in this unique setting, is that they would be entered into the Guinness World Records books.

I kept in touch with Paul and in 2024 he came to the Alpine Run Project graduation and really understood and appreciated it. Then in early 2025, he reached out and said, 'John, do you want to run the World's Deepest Marathon with us?' I said, 'I'd love to, but I'm doing another event the weekend before and I'm not going to be able to race again the following weekend, because I'll fuck myself up. How about I get a couple of young kids from the Alpine Run Project to come and do it?'

Paul could have easily got top triathletes or marathon runners to come, but he didn't want that, because, as I said before, BecomingX's ethos is: 'Anybody can achieve extraordinary things.' He agreed, so we then put an application form out to our Alpine Run cohort and had 15 who applied for it. We then shortlisted that to two: Toni and Claire. Paul then called up and said, 'I've got the money to take the girls. To give you a ballpark figure, it costs $30,000 per entry.' Without Paul, there's no doubt whatsoever that Toni and Claire couldn't have afforded that 30 grand. I said to them, 'These are real influencers. They're worth billions and they don't boast about their money. Yes, you'll get a certificate for being part of the Guinness World Record, but it's more the people you'll meet. They will open up doors for you that nobody else can open.'

They both completed the marathon on 25 October 2025, running in 72 per cent humidity in temperatures of 24°C, in total silence and complete darkness, with only their head torches for light. Running down there with no music or crowds for stimulus forces resilience and I'm so proud of them for finishing it. As far as the opportunity goes, I just see myself as a bridge, helping to take them from one world to another. Then it's all down to them.

Hitting a vision of 100,000 Alpine Run Project participants by, say, 2027 or 2028 is a bold statement, but nothing is impossible. However, you only do that by getting into the education system, fundamentally looking at classroom-based activities to engage students, but also by getting the runners to participate in cultures and terrain outside the UK. Another similar opportunity that came my way to present to the Alpine Run participants was the

Burj2Burj 2026, which is Dubai's iconic half marathon. Here's how that came about.

I was at the Sport Beach event in Cannes in June 2025 and I'd been strategically placed to sit next to a really lovely guy called Tom Otton at a lunch. He's a founder and CEO of Create Group and runs the Burj2Burj. The intention was for us to chat about doing something in the future with his event, which was exactly the sort of opportunities I wanted my runners to get involved in.

Move forward to August 2025 and I was on a call with a guy from the Dubai tourism board, and they wanted me to run the Burj2Burj half marathon in February 2026. We had a discussion and, not long after they agreed to put a sum of money into the Alpine Run Project, for me to bring out five kids for the race. That would include getting flown in, put up in hotels and all the treats. For these kids, who have grown up on council estates in London, Manchester or Birmingham, to go out to the Middle East, spend three or four days, run a half marathon and get to experience that different culture is brilliant.

In the future, my intention will be to continue to open as many doors as I can, give them those opportunities with some guidance and then leave them to do the magic. I want to be able to hand this over to someone else to keep growing this little project. Same with all the projects. I want to be mentioned less and less in the media and want more and more focus to be on the kids and them growing the project.

Chapter 23

Eyes Forward, Feet on the Ground

'The only difference between the saint and the sinner is that every saint has a past, and every sinner has a future.'

—Oscar Wilde

THE LAST time I saw my uncle, Micky McAvoy, was in 2004 when I was in Spain and I spoke to him a couple of times when I was in prison with my mate Roger. I first found out he'd died in 2023 through a cousin who had gone round the house and seen him dead. Because of my profile, over the years a lot of people add two and two together, come up with five and think my uncle Micky was my dad, mainly because we looked so similar. When he died, one of the red-top newspapers found my mum's address and went round there hoping to do an interview with me about him. That was never going to happen.

I was also asked to take part in a documentary that talked about my uncle, and I categorically said no. Then when the documentary came out, journalists started piping up, emailing me about the documentary, wanting my opinion, and once again I shut them down. I'll be honest, though, it's not the first time I've been asked to do stuff like that relating to my past, but each and every time I shut them down and refuse to give them any of my time.

However, when these type of shows come out, I watch them, simply because I need to be aware of the content. The recent one that came out in 2025 was awful. Let's leave it at that. What I would say, though, from a personal perspective, is how it made me reflect again on where I was in my life. Watching these men in their 60s and 70s is where I definitely didn't want to be. I'd previously been absorbed by the callousness and flippant nature of human life being extinguished. My life has shifted in a different direction and I don't put any blame on my uncle or anyone else when I was growing up. I felt so loved by everyone and that way of life was normal for them, and then it became normal for me. I don't feel any resentment towards them; I just think I'm very fortunate that I got out when I did.

Am I complacent of my freedom a few years down the line? No. I think about this a lot, most days. I have an immense amount of gratitude for the life I've got. I'd never take it for granted, and now I'd never ever compromise on my freedom. To me, that is the most important thing ever, even to the point of wanting to stay on my own on occasions, because I don't want to compromise what I want to do and when I want to do it. I don't want to have to ask people's permission to do things. For me, freedom is absolutely paramount to my existence on planet Earth until the day I die.

I obviously love sport for what it's been able to give me as a life and the people and friendships it's brought into my life; that will last forever. Of course, we all have our up and down days, and we get frustrated, but you have to catch yourself, reset and say, 'You know what? It could be so much worse. You're free and you've got water and food. You're good.' You have to be mindful about these things, and when you drift off into a hole where you're dealing with difficult people or situations, and things aren't going the way you want them to go, you can easily slip into negative mindset and you just have to catch yourself.

Living in the mountains has profoundly changed me, because you can really detach yourself. It's not a case of becoming a hermit, but I've gone through times where you're in this profound size of nature, you can go out for days and not see people and you realise you're just this tiny little microscopic creature in this vast space. When you're submerged in it, everything else just becomes white noise.

Since being released, I've visited HMP Feltham about 30 times, Lowdham Grange about ten times, the Scrubs four times and, when I'm in the UK nowadays, I'll sometimes drive to Belmarsh or Sudbury prisons and sit outside the front gates. It's easy to drift off, thinking about the past, but for me it's the opposite. I think about how far I've come.

For the first couple of years, I was so single-minded to be different that I wouldn't watch a programme on television that had crime, listen to it on the radio or read about it on the internet. Now I'm happy to be exposed to that world, because I'm approaching it from a different perspective. In fact, since coming out of prison, I've tried to expose myself as much as possible to youngsters who are getting close to entering that world and speaking to as many government organisations as possible to help spread the word that there's more positive roads you can take in life.

In January 2023, I posted on Instagram, saying, 'If someone said to me 10 years ago I would one day speak at the United Nations I don't think I would have even believed them.' My friend Ian Orton worked for the International Labour arm of the UN, and he said, 'Would you come in and talk to my team?' Obviously, I said yes. When you go into the building, you can't help but be in awe of the surroundings. I love history, and you've got all these paintings on the wall and all these international flags. You walk down this big blue carpet and there's all these dates about how the UN started and what they've been doing since.

Talking about my journey in sport to the International Labour Organization emphasised the importance of the work they do, why it's so important to give back in society and how to protect those individuals by promoting social justice and recognising human and labour rights, which is what they major at. On that particular occasion in 2023, I posted a photo, and the girl standing next to me is Toby Hunter's daughter, Gracie. She wanted to work in the UN, so I asked Toby whether she wanted to come with me, then got clearance from the UN. Gracie is a super-bright girl who impressed every single person attending that event. It's a great full-circle moment. Toby helped me when I was trying to navigate the corporate world many years before, and here I was, in a position to do a small thing for his daughter. I ended up going to the UN on multiple occasions. It's all well and good me being invited to these events and occasions, but if I don't make an active effort to try to help others along the way, then I've failed in my own journey.

As far as competing and winning goes, I'm not concerned about how fast I now go or who I beat; it's all about being the best version of myself. If you attach your identity and self-worth to winning, you're walking down a very dangerous road and could fall into a very deep, dark hole that you'll struggle to get out of as you get older. Athletes don't win all the time. It's like what Michael Jordan once said about missing more shots than he scored, but that failure over and over again is why he succeeded.

Physical prowess eventually leaves all of us as time catches up with us. As long as I can look over my shoulder after crossing the finishing line knowing I got the best out of myself on that day, that works for me. When you've bad race days, and mentally you're great but your body doesn't turn up, you can't beat yourself up and let that fester.

At the time of writing, I'm in my early 40s, thankfully still in good health and competing regularly. I often get asked these days, 'What will you do when you can't compete at that level anymore, and what will your focus in life and purpose be?' Although I became an athlete, I never intended to be one. My journey into sport has never been about that. My dream as a kid wasn't to become a professional athlete, and the same goes for when I was in prison doing cell circuits. I just did something I love to do and I still exercise every day for the love of it. The day I stop exercising will be the day I'm buried. Yes, I will get slower at what I do, but I accept that. I will always use my body, and even though my motivation will differ, I'll always be able to adapt and still find something physically that I love doing. At the moment, I can ride my bike, beat people half my age and drop them on a mountain climb, and the same goes for running. Sport for me is a way of life that will never end.

It's not like I have a sell-by date. I love doing exercise and being outside with nature. It's like meditation, which is why I like training on my own so much. Being in the middle of nowhere with nobody knowing where I am, with my phone on aeroplane mode.

As for the legacy I'd like to leave, I need to take the timeline right back to explain. When my dad died, before I was even born, that did something to me. It made me ferociously ambitious, because I knew I wasn't going to live forever. I had this intoxicating drive of legacy and not only wanting to achieve something significant in my life but being remembered for it. Unfortunately, there was no Alpine Run Projects, or Open Doors around for me to channel my ambition and energy into.

When you put yourself in a position like an armed robbery, you sometimes end up dealing with the unknown. I know many people who've gone out to do a job without the intention of hurting anyone, then someone's jumped on them and they've killed that person and they're in prison for life, for a minimum of 35 years. At the time, you don't see that outcome. You dehumanise the people and get fixated on the money, and the people in front of you are just in the way of you getting that money. My stepdad used to say about firearms, 'You don't need them. You just need your voice. You need to be able to direct people and tell them what to do.' He always used to pride himself on not ever having anything on him. He could control people just by speaking to them.

If I hadn't gone to prison, I probably would have carried on committing crimes to a much higher level. When I was a young kid, they gave me the nickname of 'Brains', because I used to memorise registration plates and I used to follow security vans all over the place knowing which day they'd drop money, how many times per week, etc. I feel embarrassed even thinking about that now, but if I hadn't got caught, I'd have progressively got worse and I'd have always wanted to make more and more money, and those connections in that criminal world allowed me to do that. Eventually I would have probably been in a prison abroad and my life would have been a cycle of massive highs and massive lows. I can look at other people's lives and, every now and then, something will pop up in the newspapers, talking about someone that I knew who are now back in prison.

I would have been in a cycle of getting out, getting big prison sentences, going back in; then, eventually, you get too old and think, 'Fuck it. I don't want to do this anymore,' as you're sitting in prison in your 60s, with kids who are 20 years old. That's how that world plays out if you normalise yourself to it and don't do anything to address it. Thankfully, the only cycles I'm involved in these days have two wheels with a mountain backdrop and don't come with a prison sentence at the end.

When I got out of prison, I was focusing on breaking records, achieving better, aiming higher. My thoughts were: *If I can do that, people will think I'm amazing and it will put to bed all the bad stuff I've ever done in my life and showing that I'm doing something more positive with my life.* You go through that journey of growth as a person and keep having different life experiences. Then you realise, nothing really matters, because a few generations down the line we're all gone. I'd like to be remembered as someone who impacted people's lives positively, through kindness and generosity, to help make their lives better. That's the plan.

HOKA
DACIA
wahoo
UTMB
17232
7399
RODE